Children of Appalachia

By Warren E. Brunner

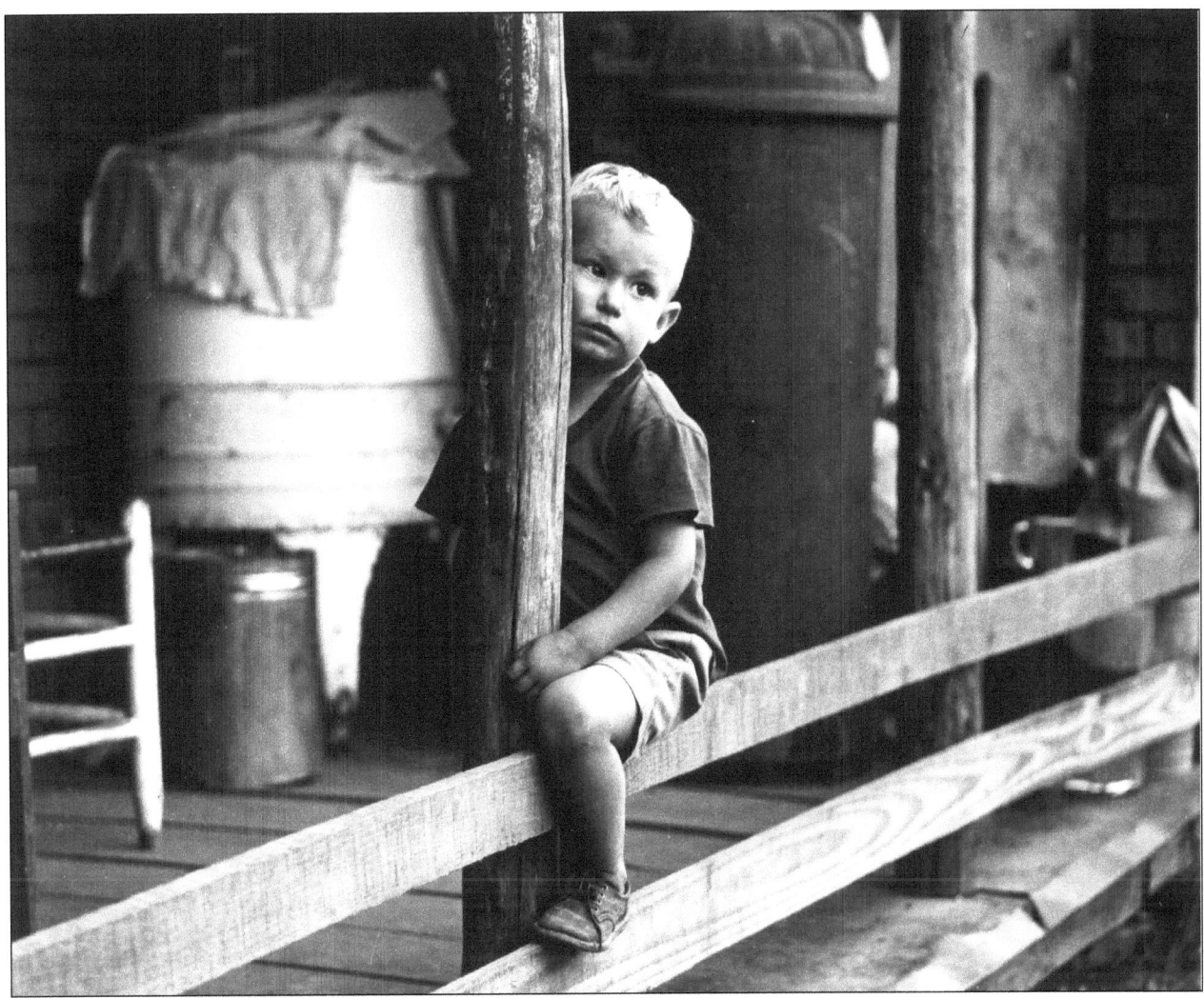

Continuing Reaction to Warren Brunner's Photograph of a Small Mountain Boy

By Grace Freeman

Solemn faced little boy
hugging that porch post,
how long will you haunt me?

I know children today
who would relish a chance to ride
that rickety wood railing
the way you do.

Modern architects
struck front porches from houses
in our part of town years ago,
substituting dens,
TV nooks and lots of shelves
for stacking comic books
and new electric games.

I feel uneasy when I look at you,
small mountain boy, and tell myself
outside the camera's range
a huge black inner tube
dangles on a rope to make a swing.

I let my fingers crop,
block out all trace of Appalachia,
frame only your face.
Still there are those eyes.

A kind heart is a fountain of gladness, making everything in its vicinity freshen into smiles.

~ Washington Irving

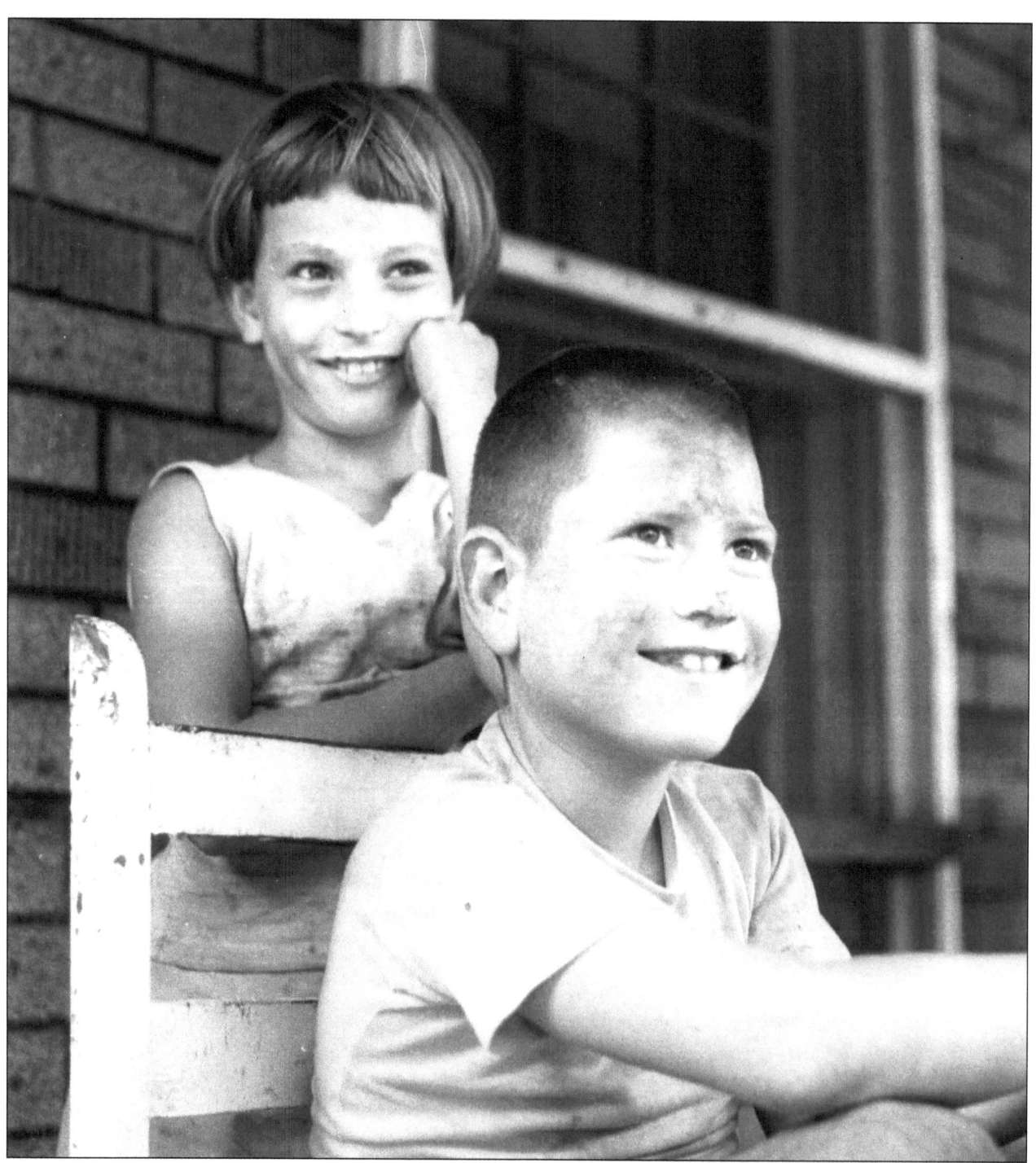

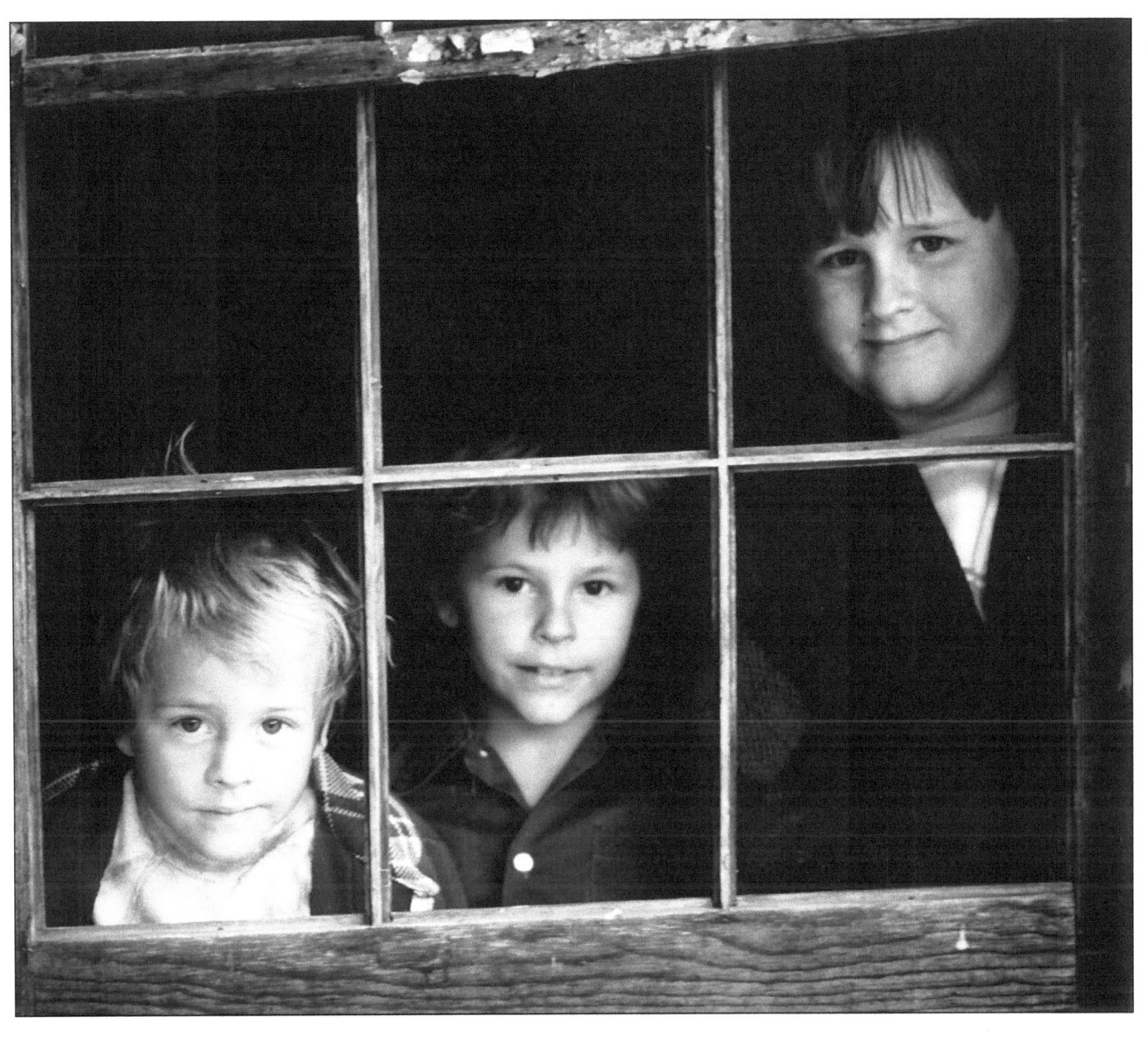

In childhood, we press our nose to the pane, looking out. In memories of childhood, we press our nose to the pane, looking in. ~ **Robert Brault**

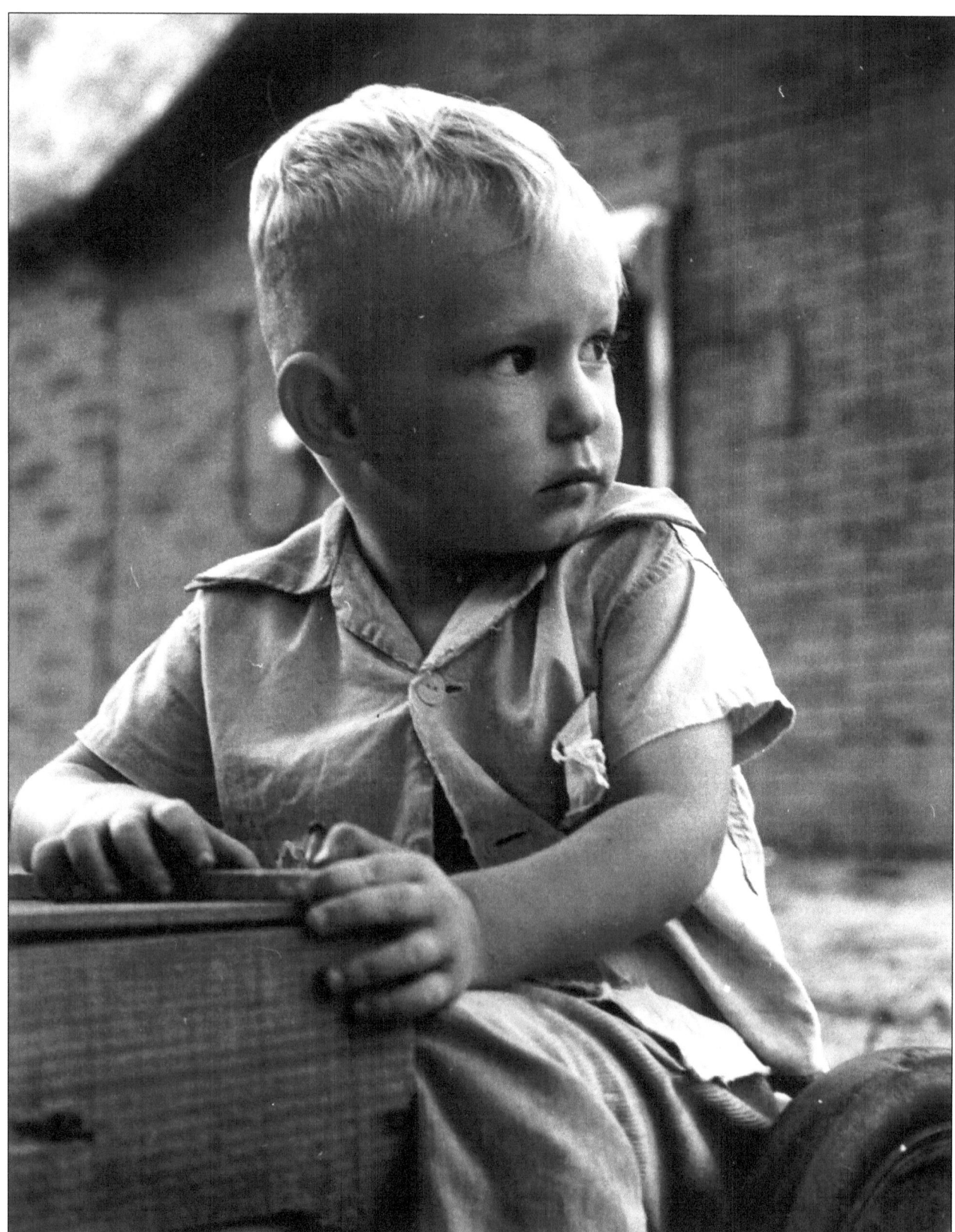

Home is the place where, when you have to go there, they have to take you in.

~ **Robert Frost**

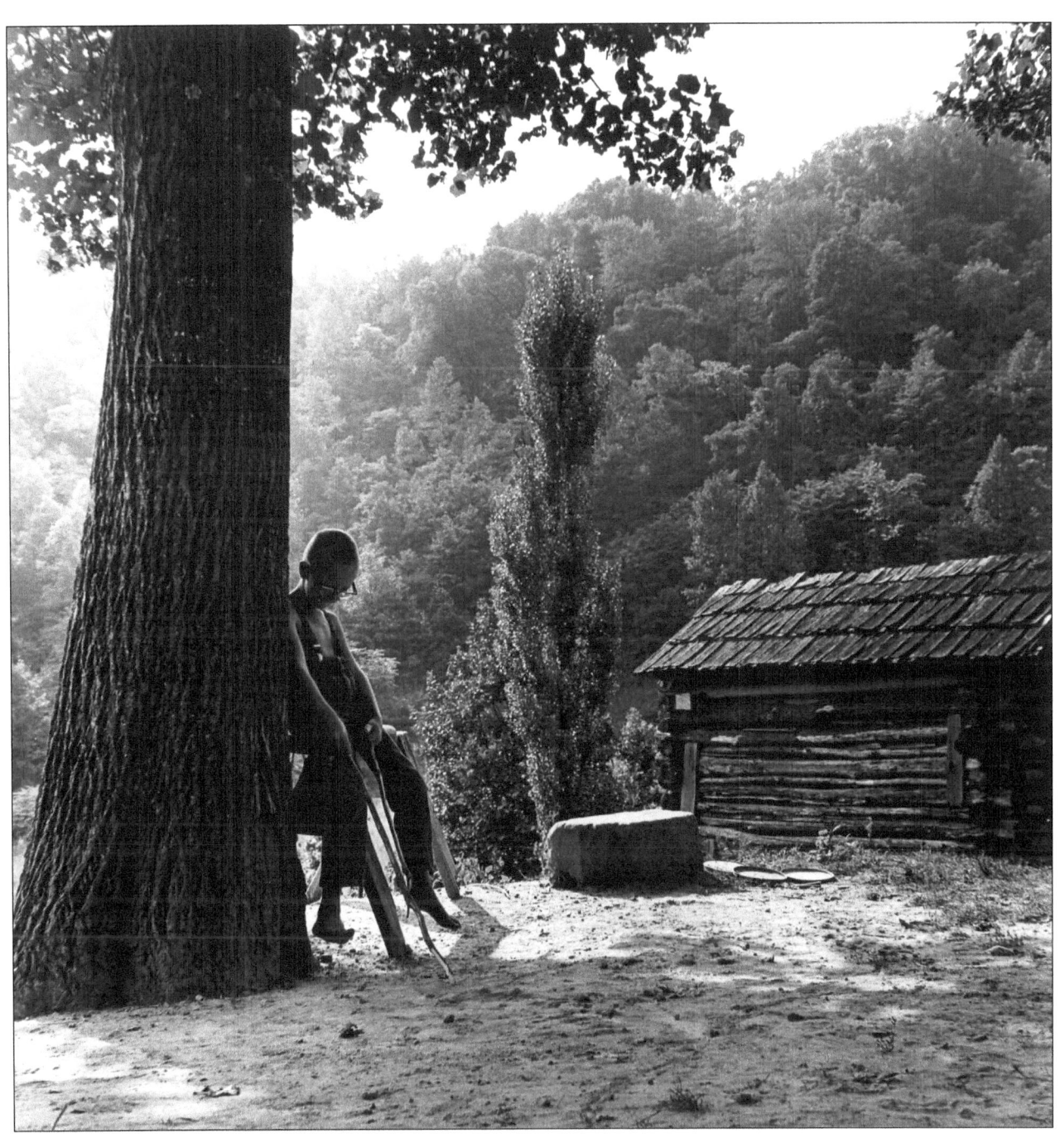

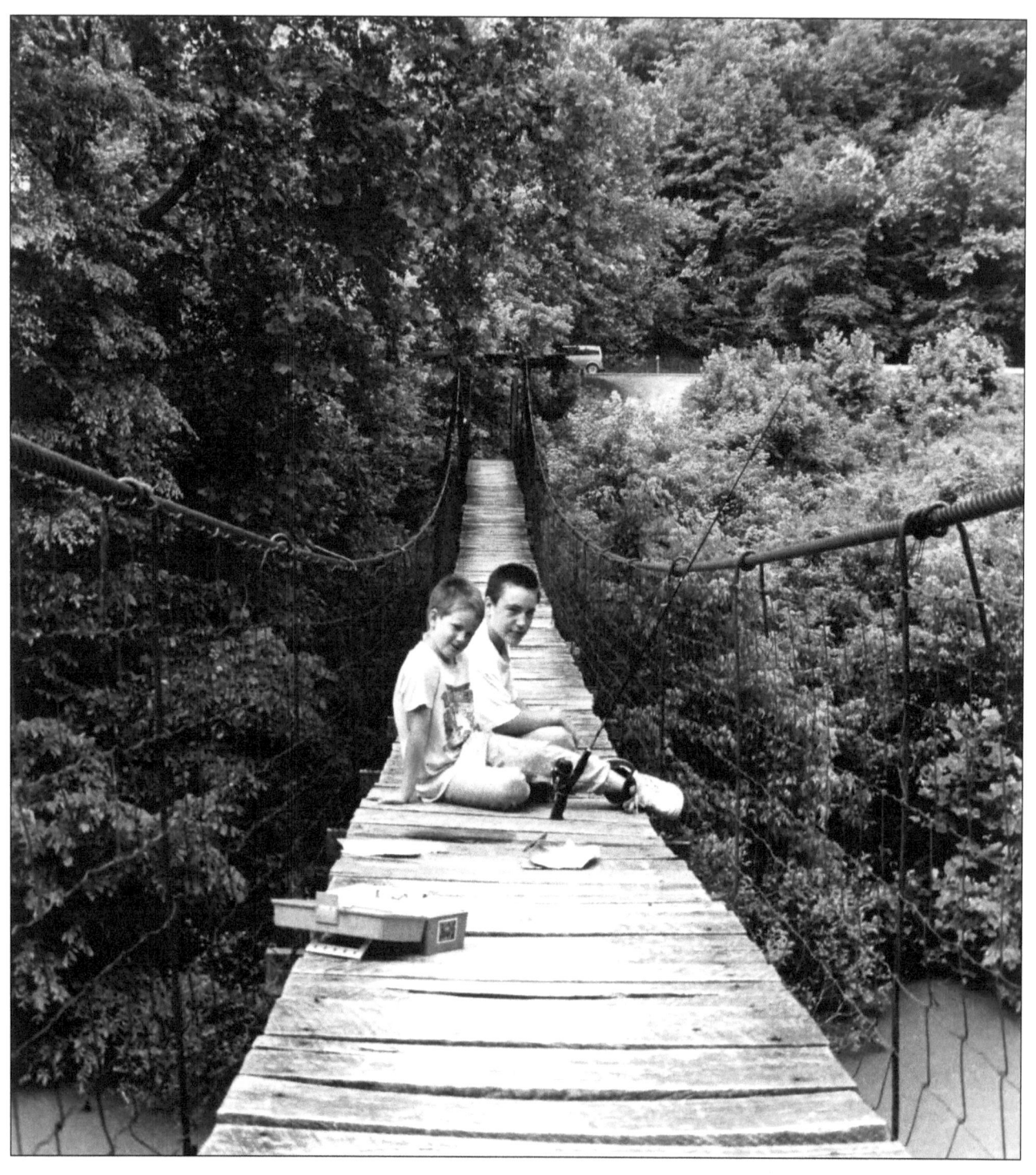

You are worried about seeing him spend his early years in doing nothing. What! Is it nothing to be happy? Nothing to skip, play, and run around all day long? Never in his life will he be so busy again. ~ **Jean-Jacques Rousseau**

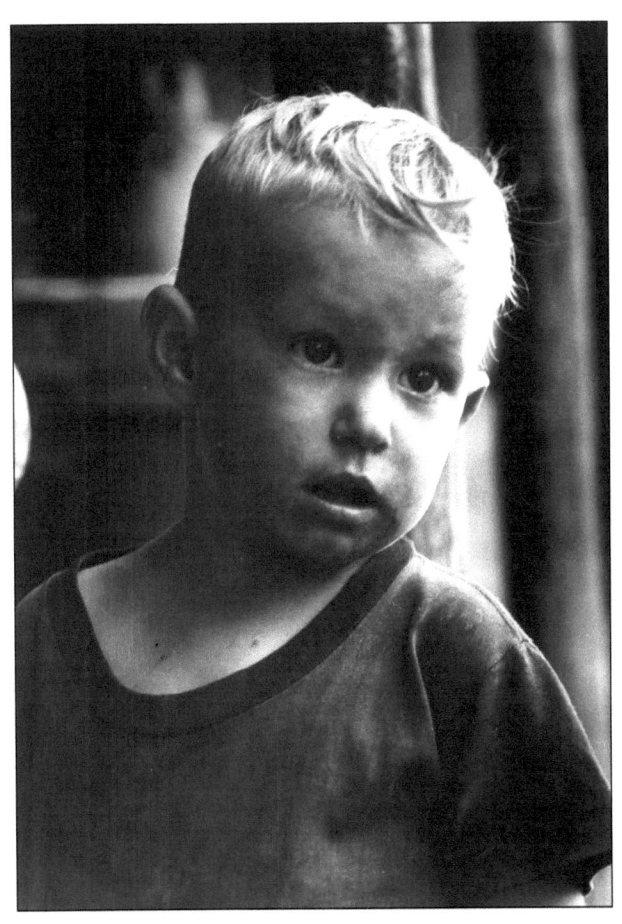
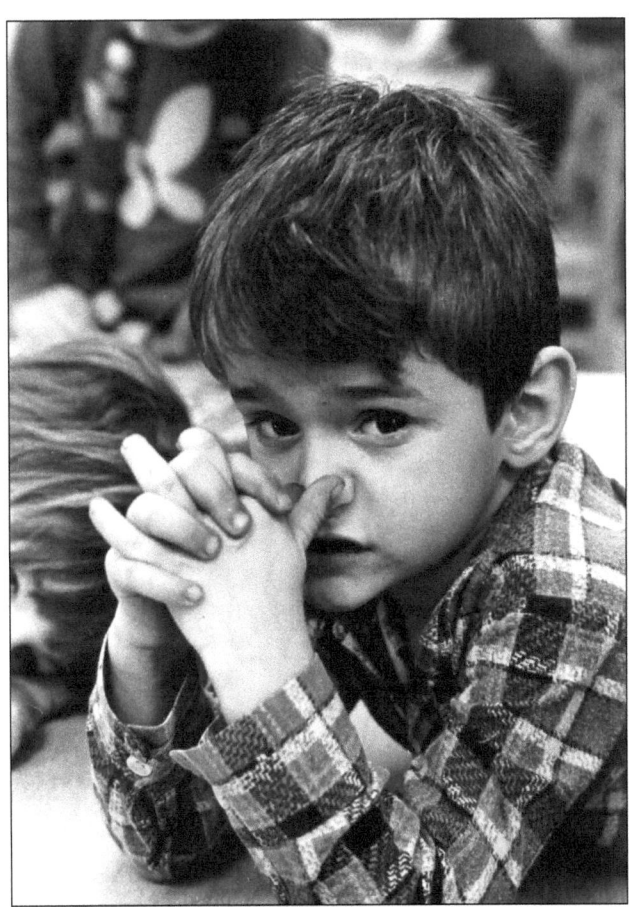

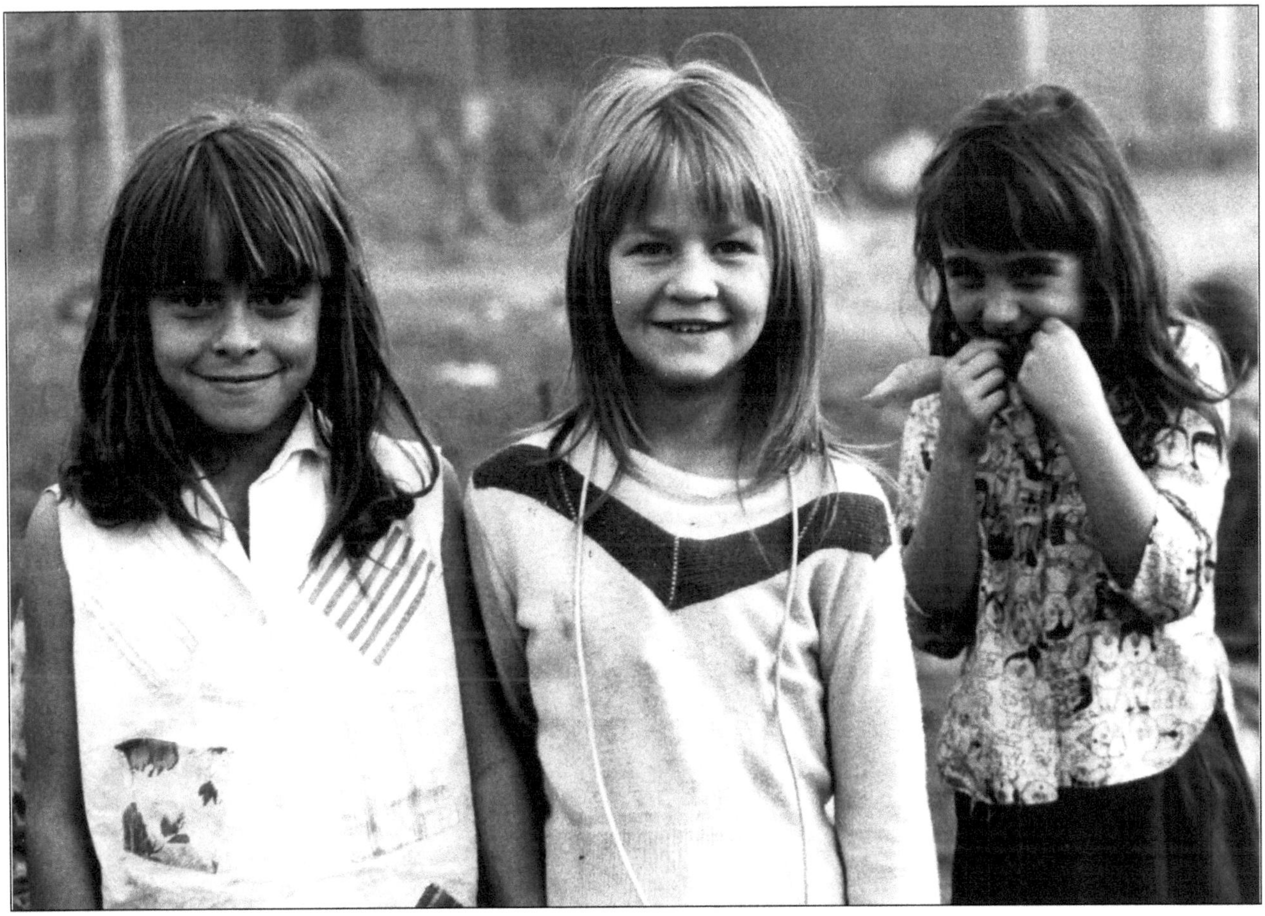

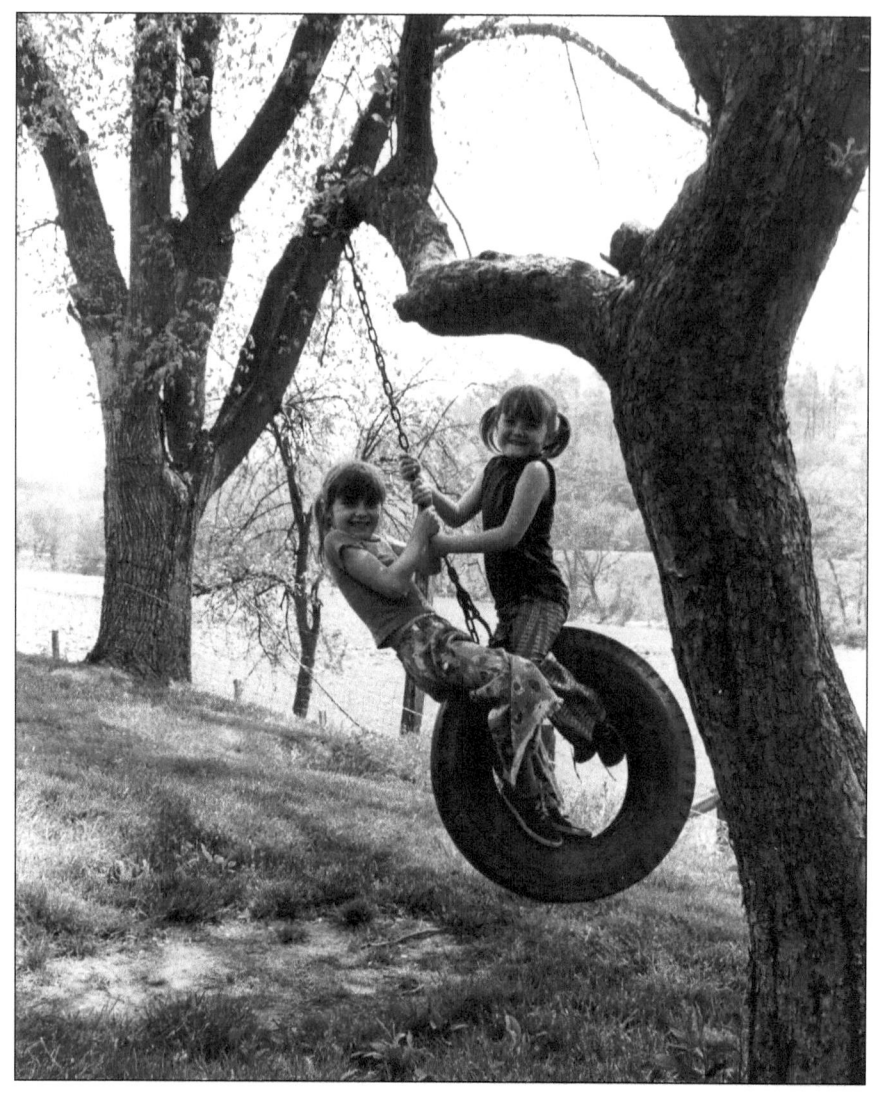

" Play is the highest
form of research.

~ Albert Einstein "

" Mirth is God's
medicine. Everybody
ought to bathe in it.
~ Henry Ward Beecher "

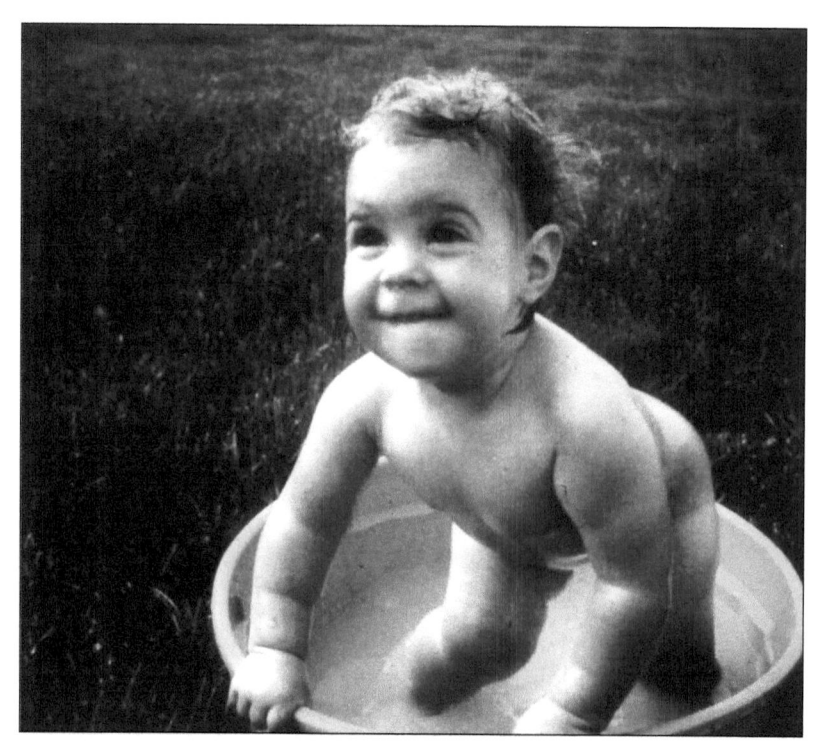

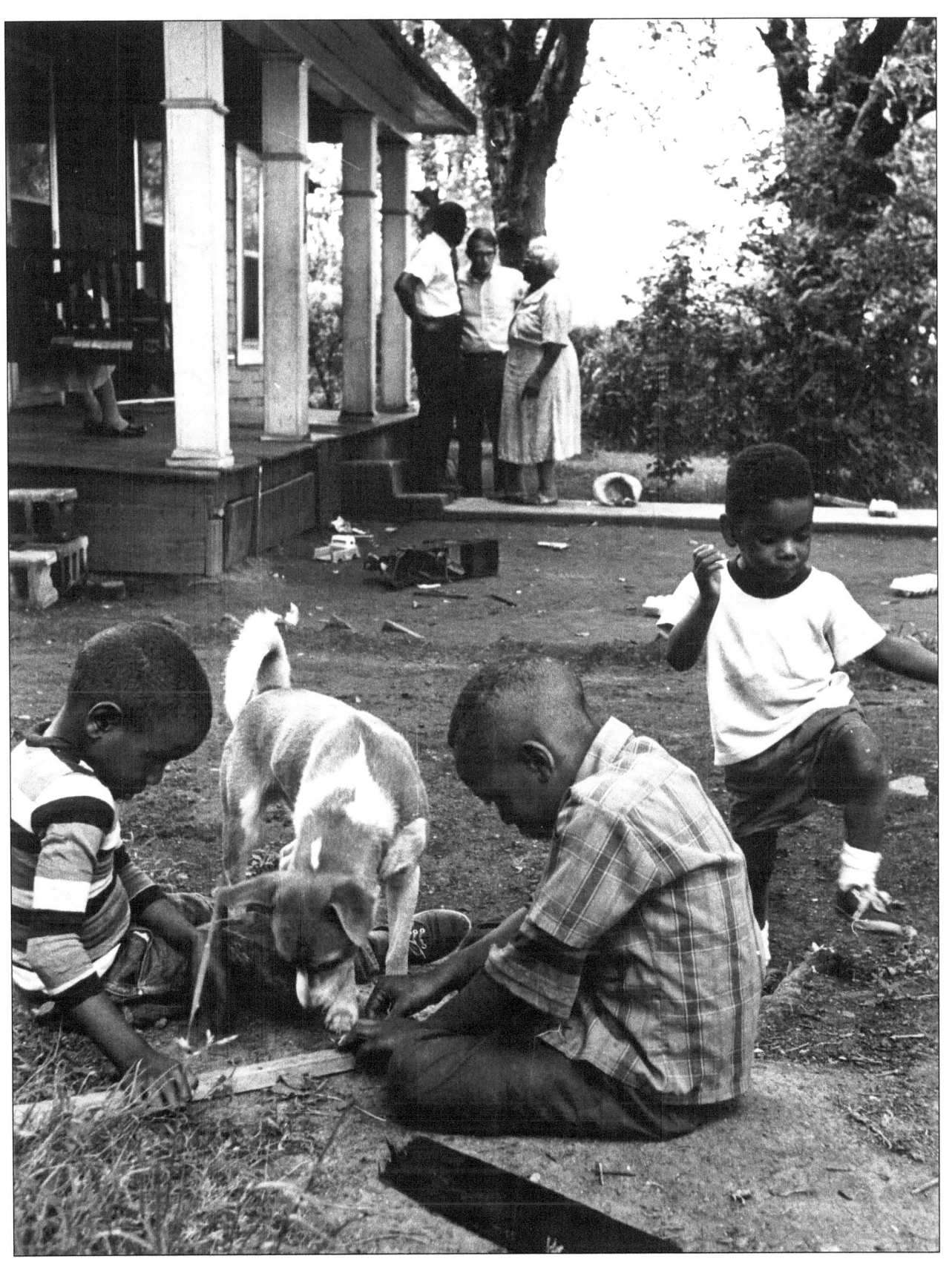

The dog was created specially for children.
He is the god of frolic. ~ Henry Ward Beecher

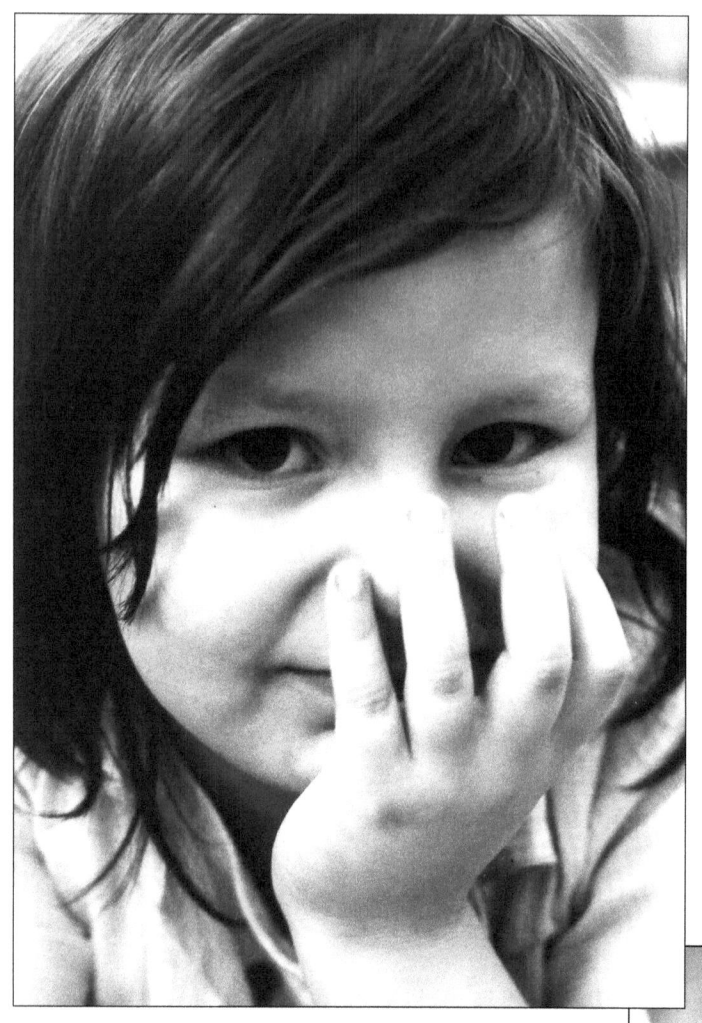

" *Laughter is the sun that drives winter from the human face.* "
~ **Victor Hugo**

" *The most interesting information comes from children, for they tell all they know and then stop.* "
~ **Mark Twain**

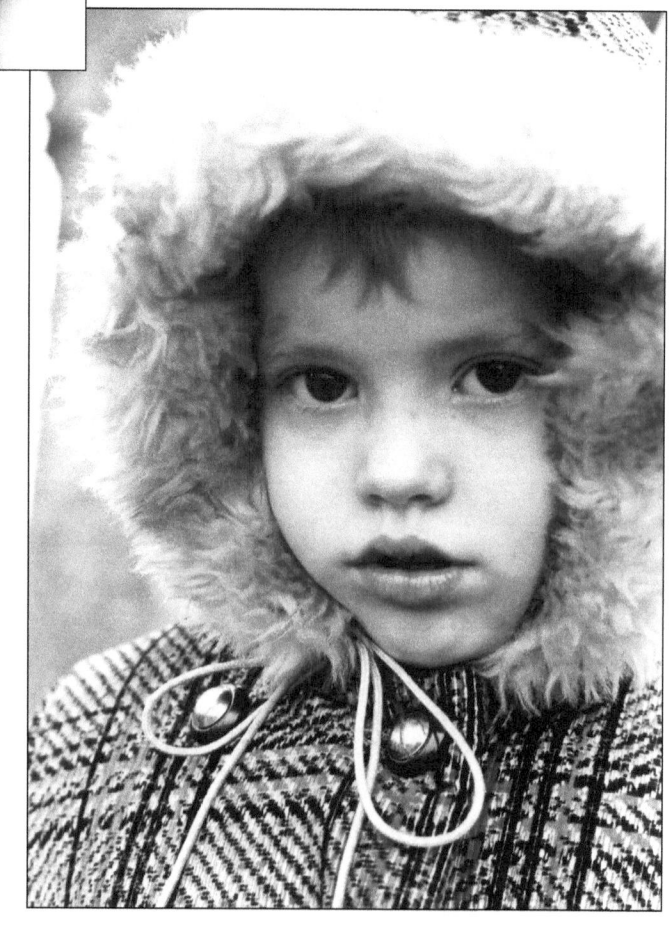

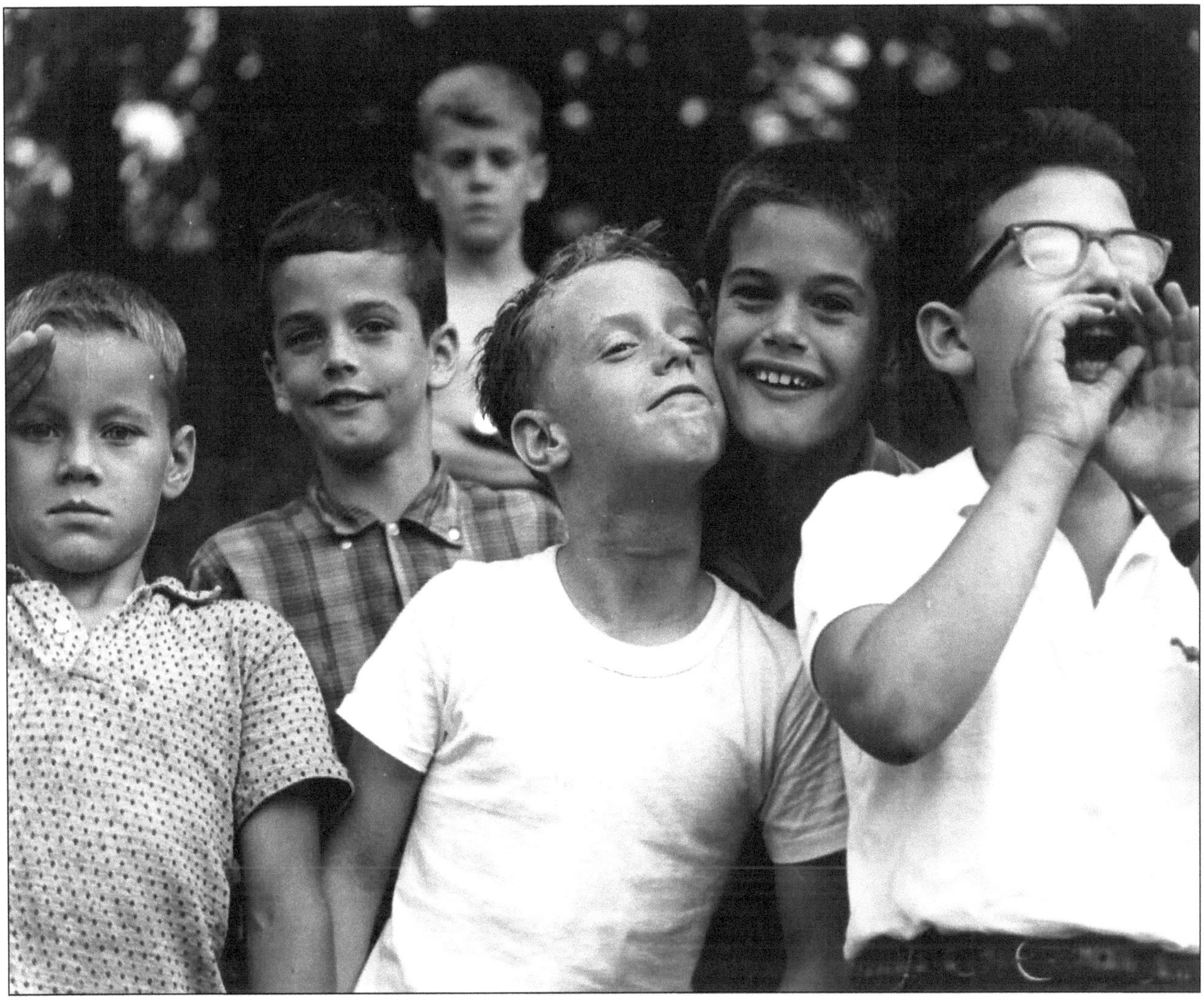

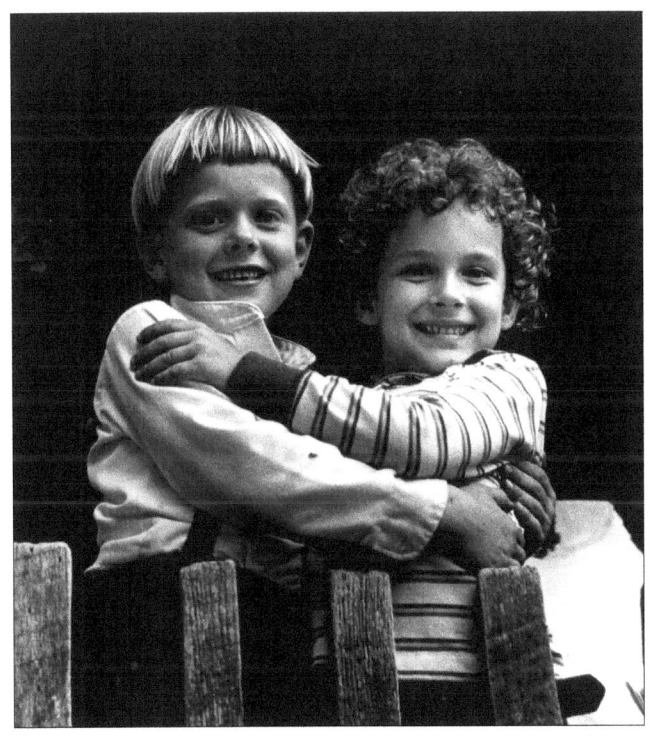

True happiness arises, in the first place, from the enjoyment of one's self, and in the next, from the friendship and conversation of a few select companions.

~ Joseph Addison

In the sweetness of friendship let there be laughter, and sharing of pleasures. For in the dew of little things the heart finds its morning and is refreshed.
~ Khalil Gibran

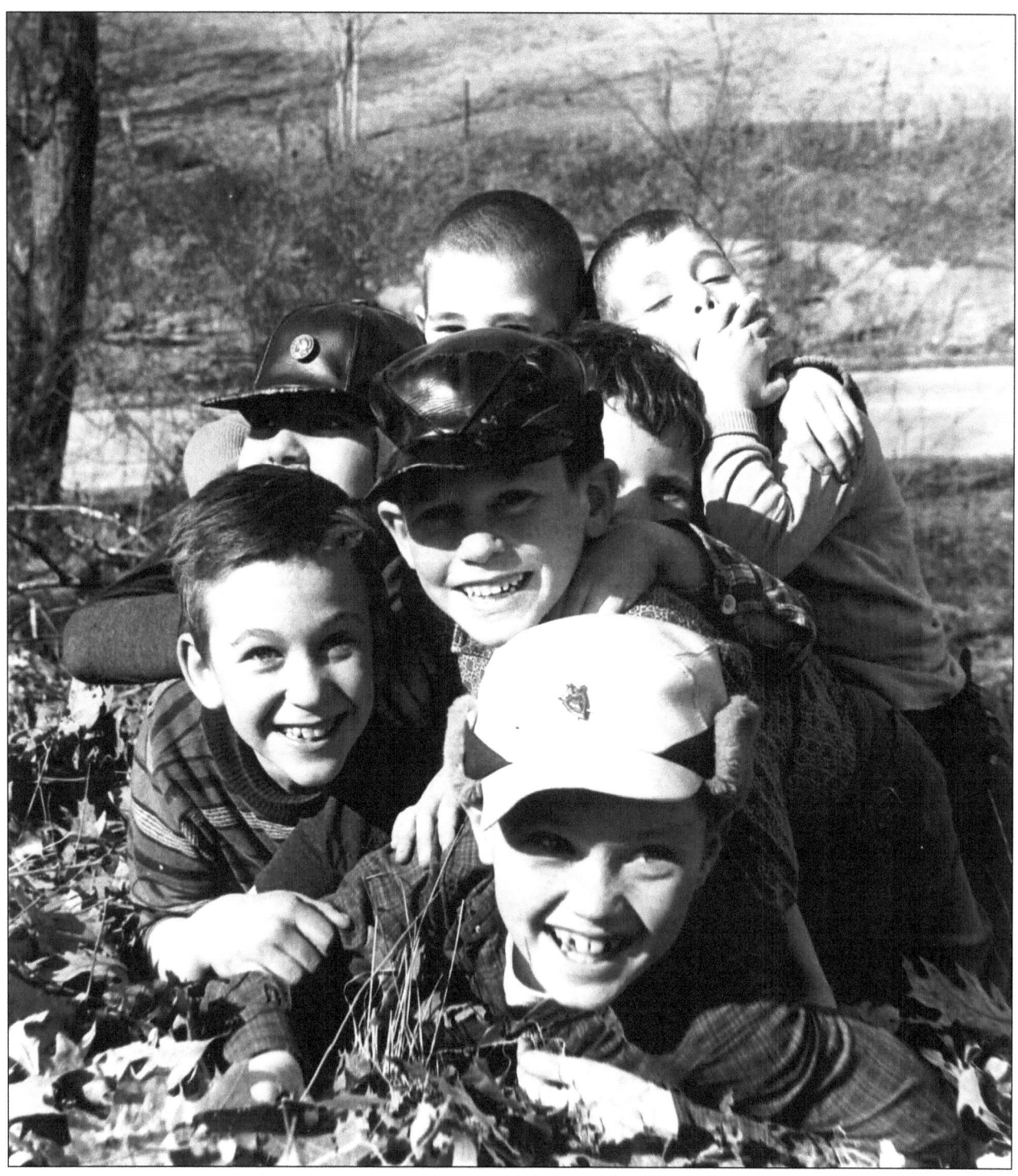

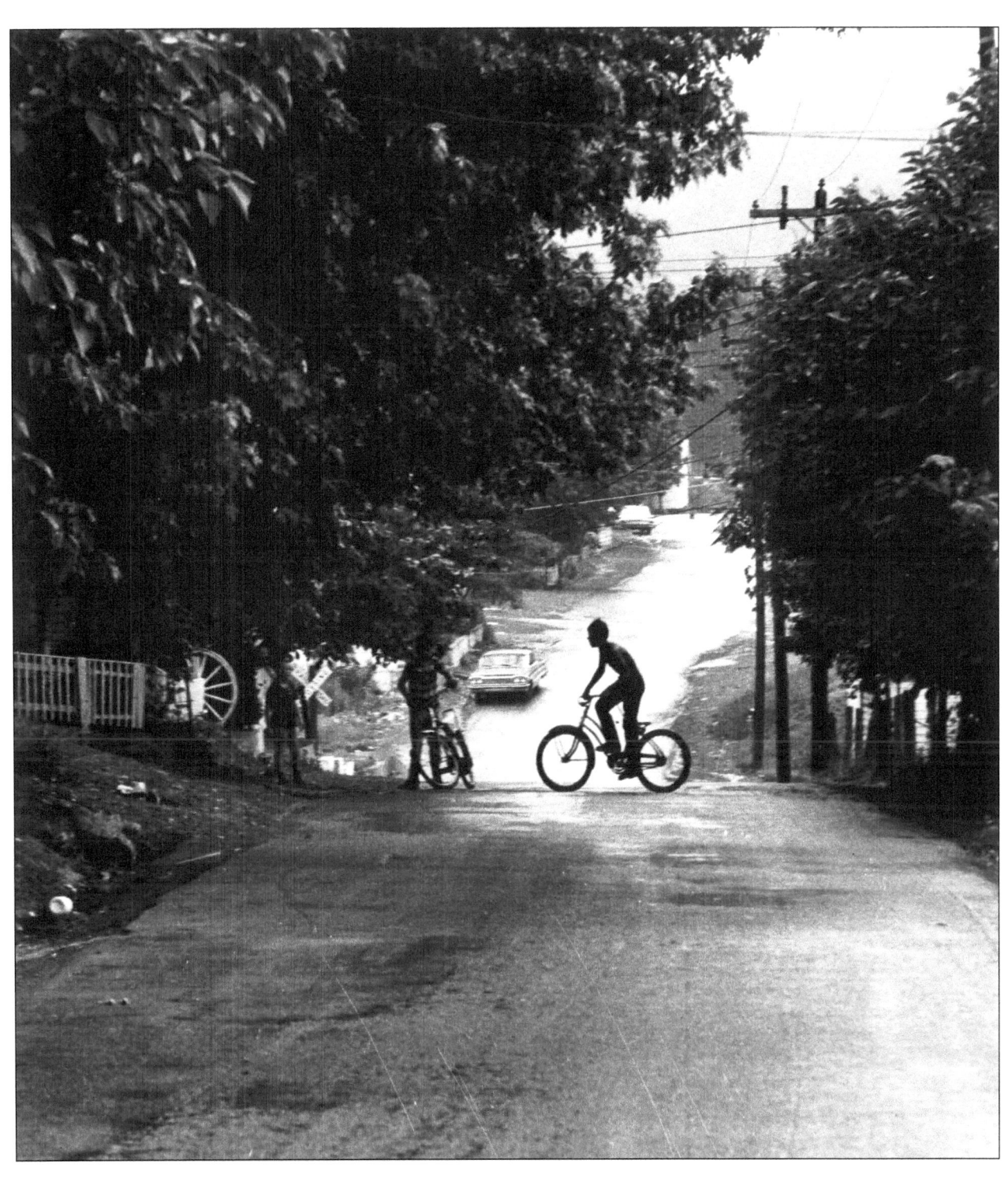

*Nothing compares to the simple pleasure
of a bike ride. ~ John F. Kennedy*

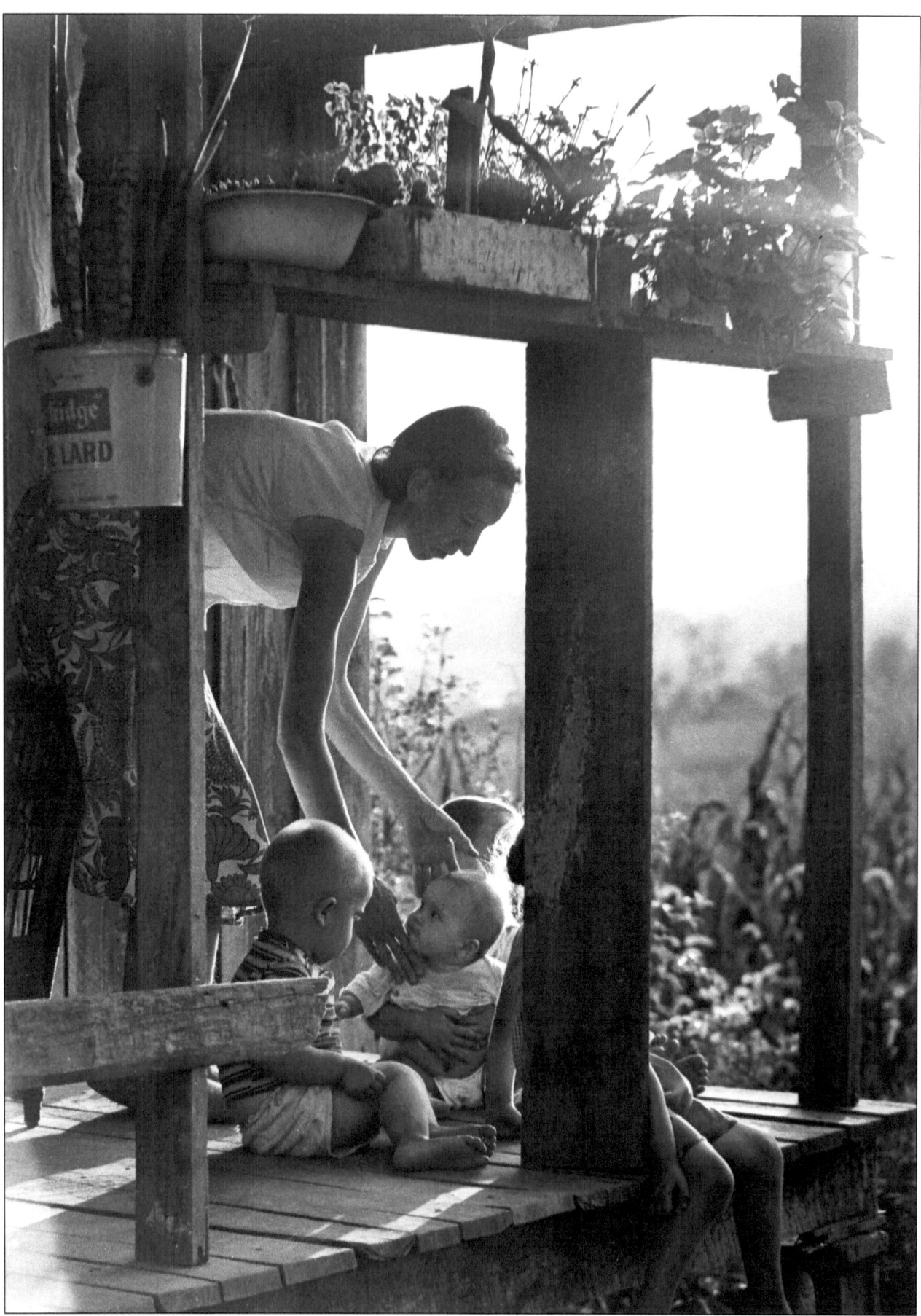

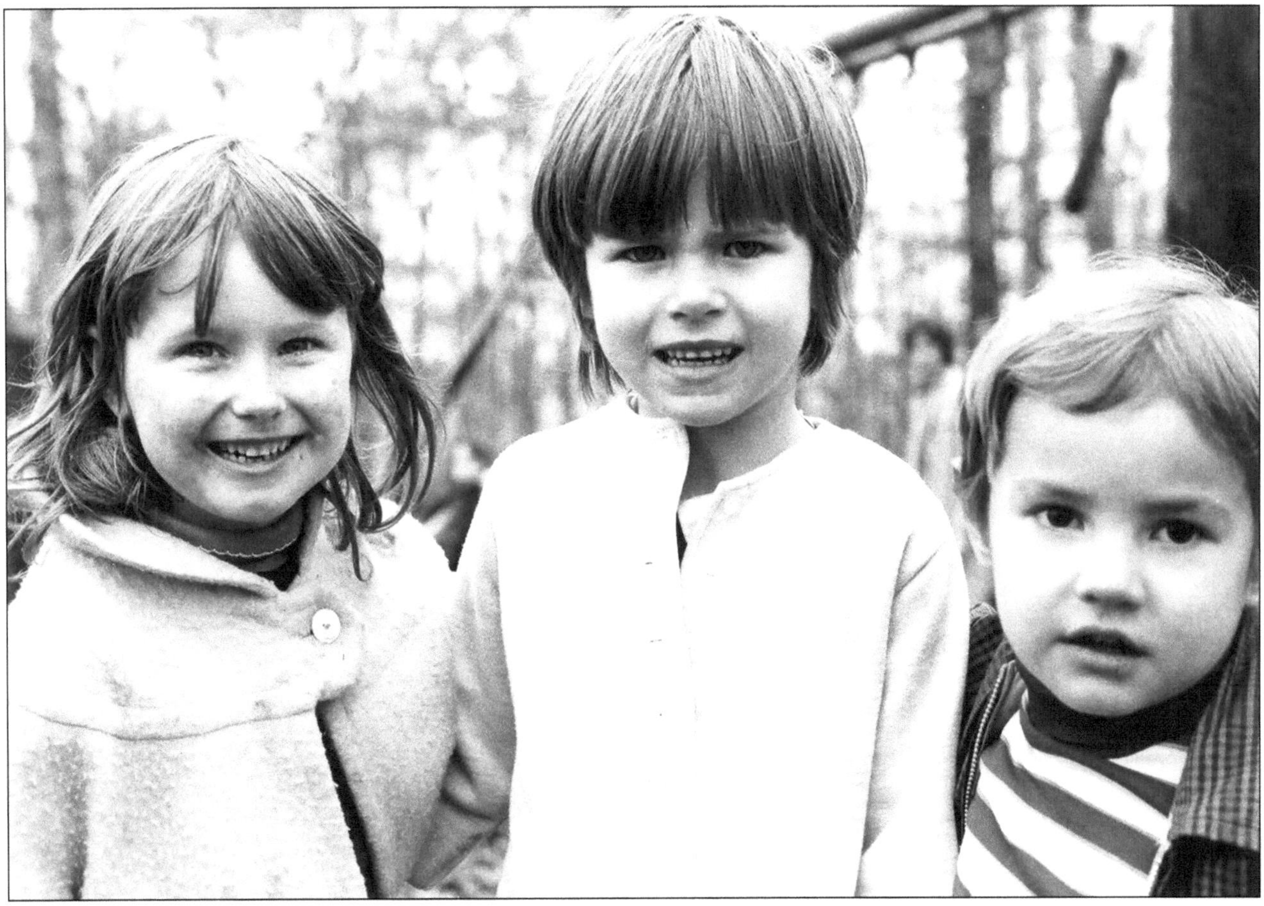

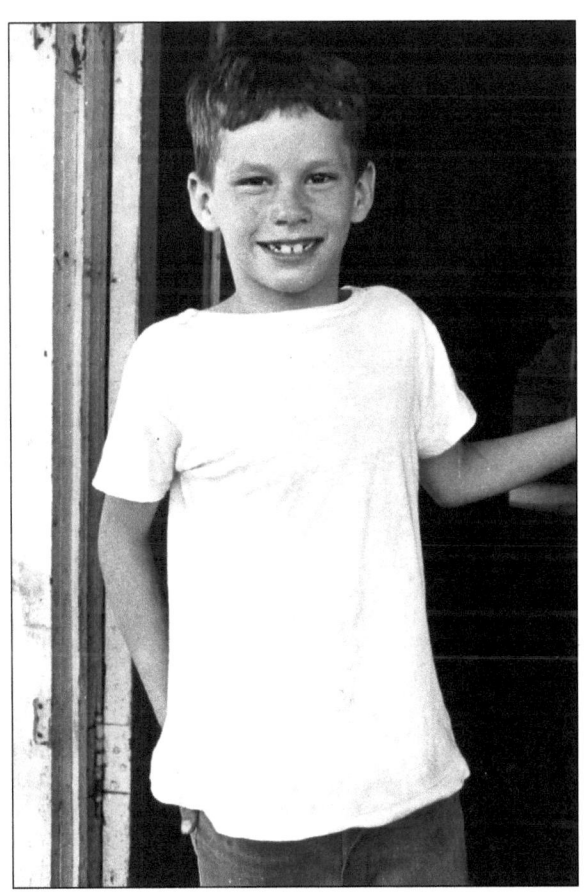

Let us be grateful to people who make us happy, they are the charming gardeners who make our souls blossom.

~ **Marcel Proust**

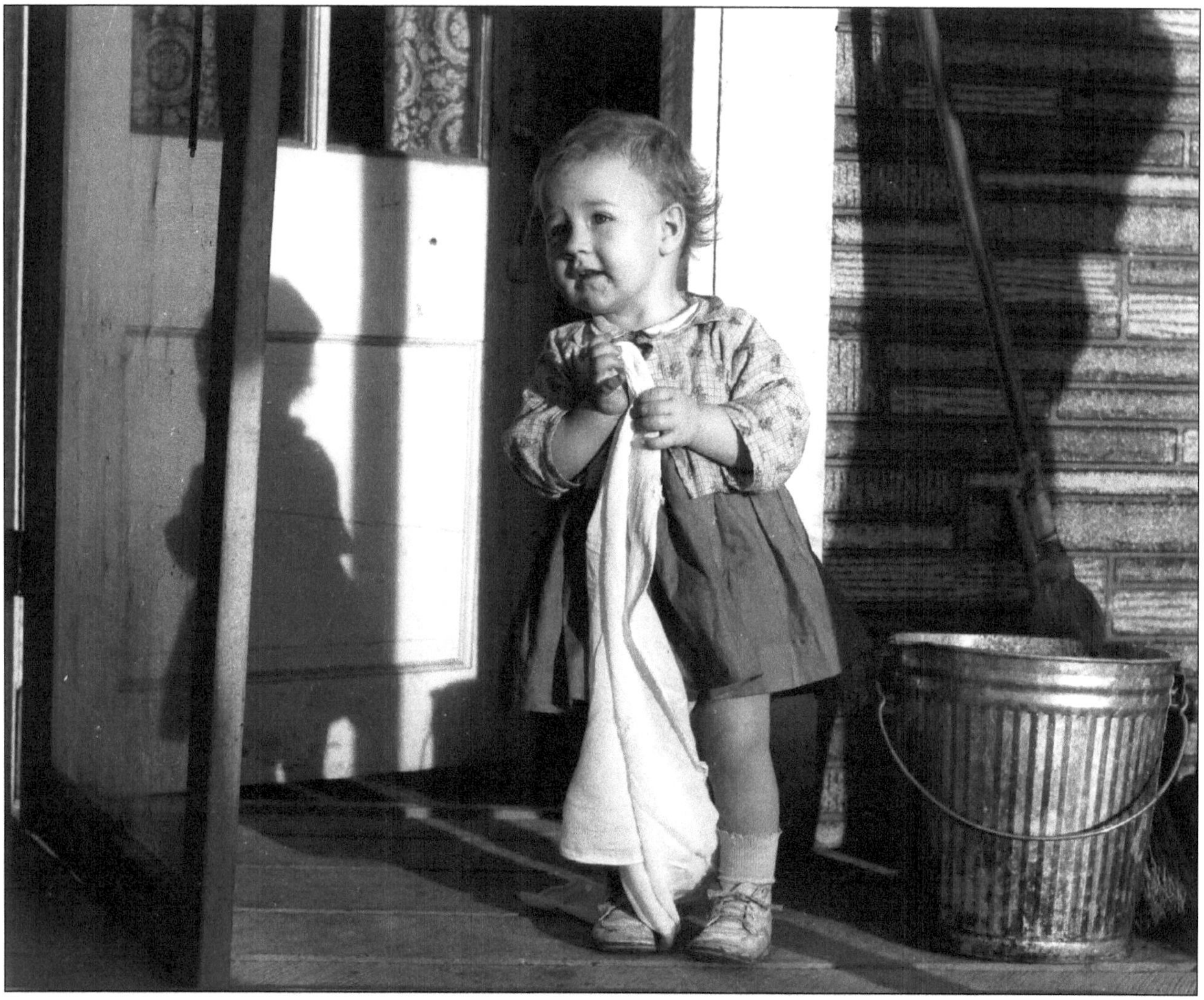

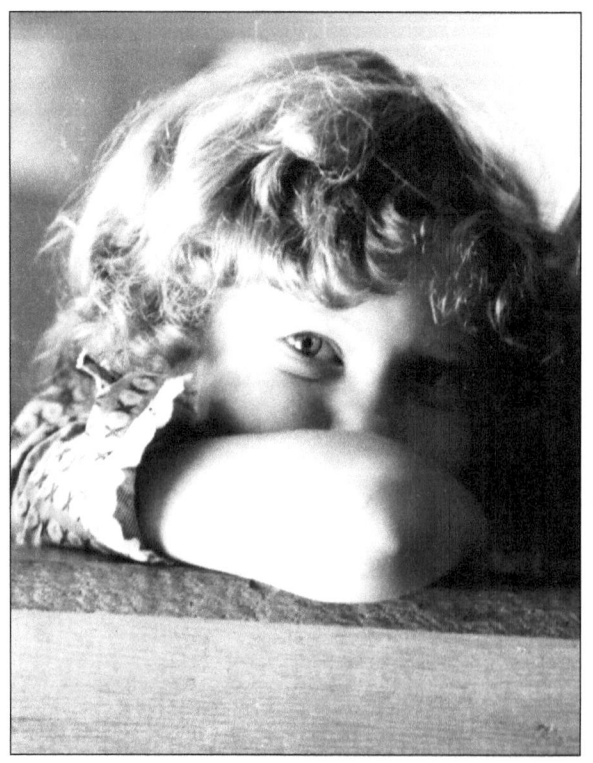

A child is a curly, dimpled lunatic. ~ **Ralph Waldo Emerson**

A happy family is but an earlier heaven.
~ **George Bernard Shaw**

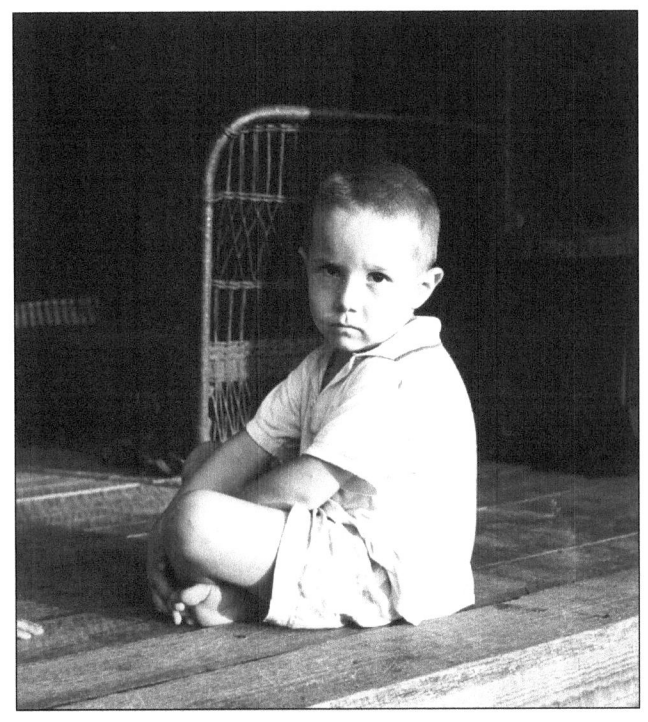

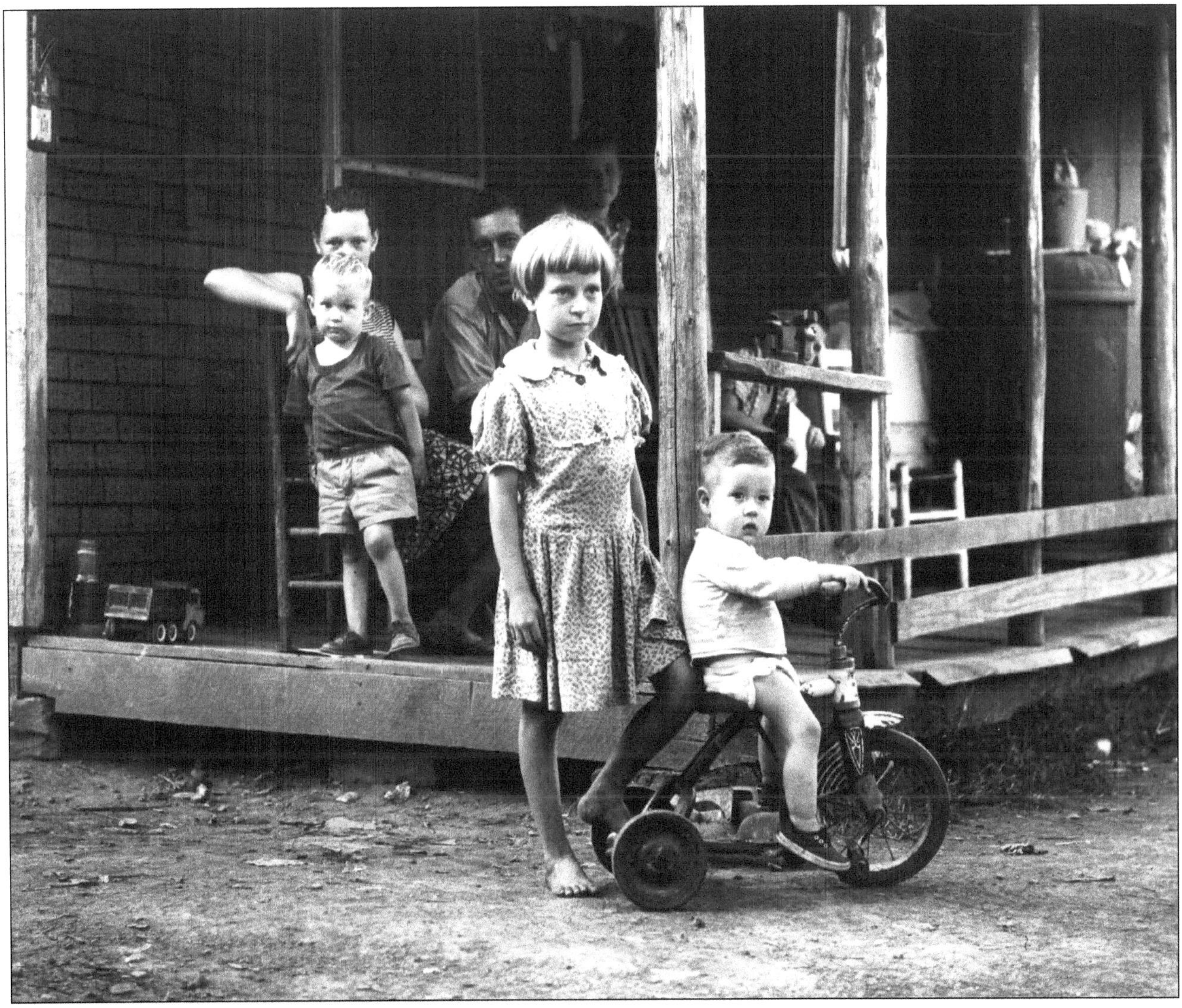

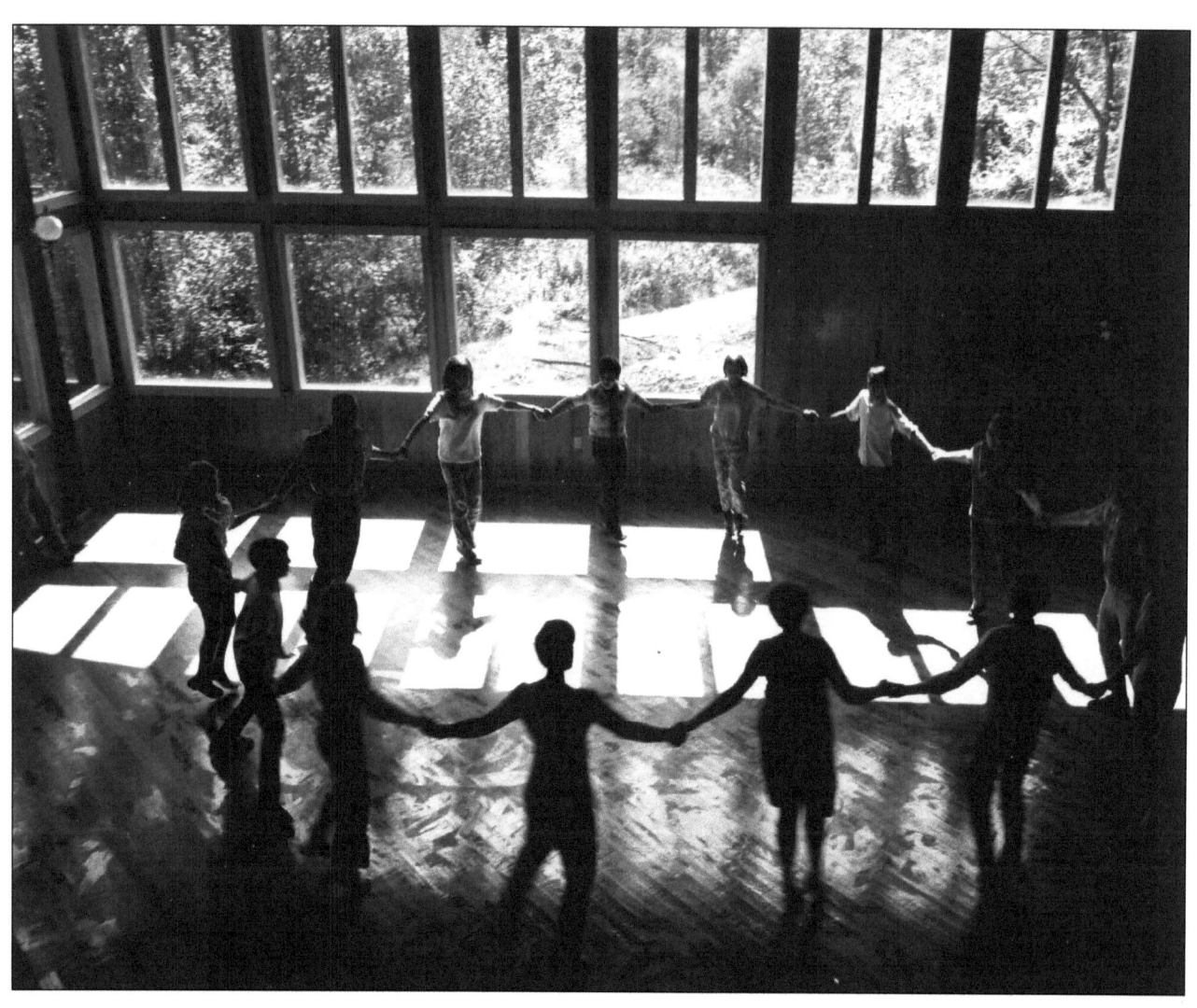

On with the dance! let joy be unconfined;
No sleep till morn, when Youth and Pleasure meet
To chase the glowing hours with flying feet.
~George Gordon, Lord Byron

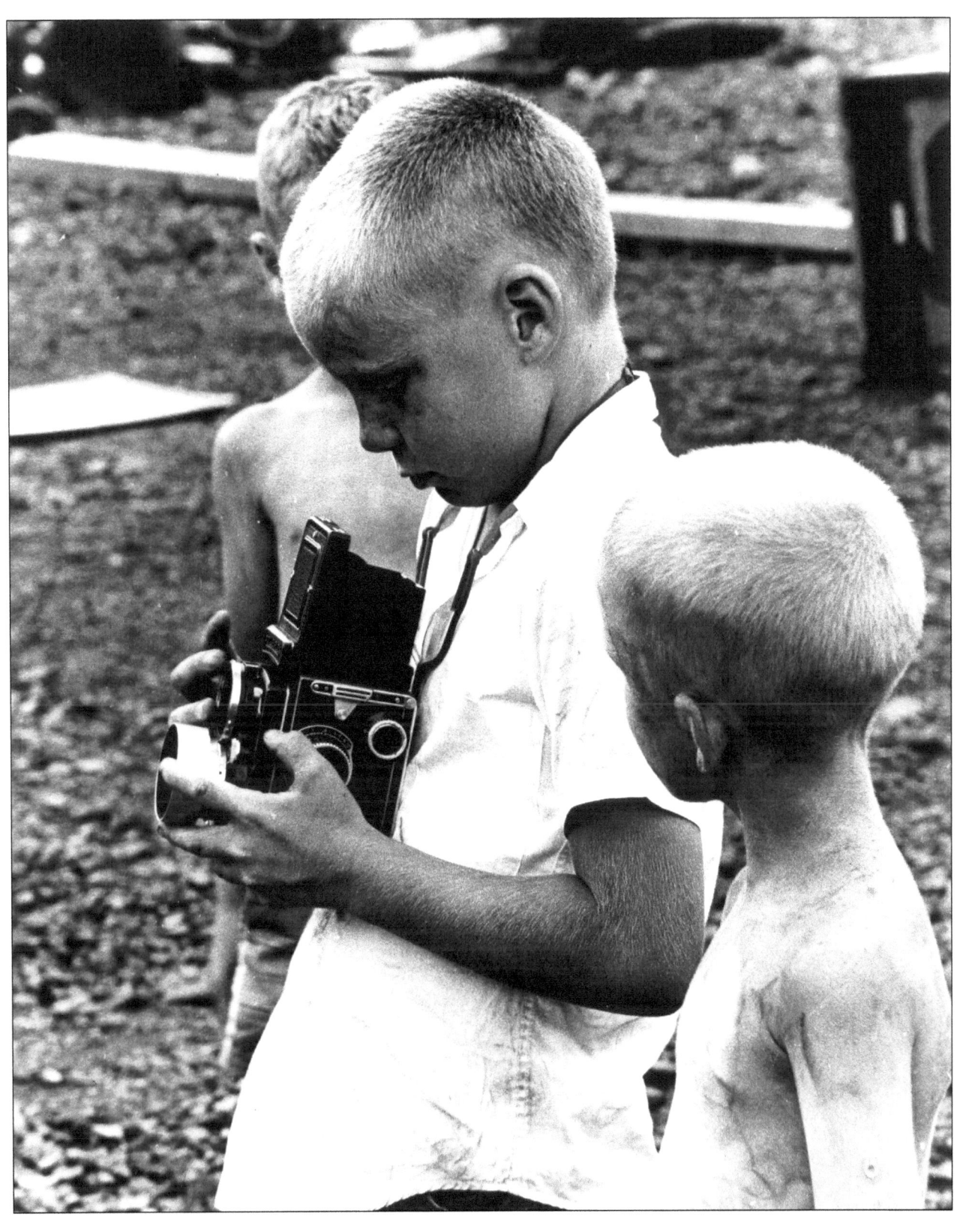

The important thing is not to stop questioning.
Curiosity has its own reason for existing.
~ **Albert Einstein**

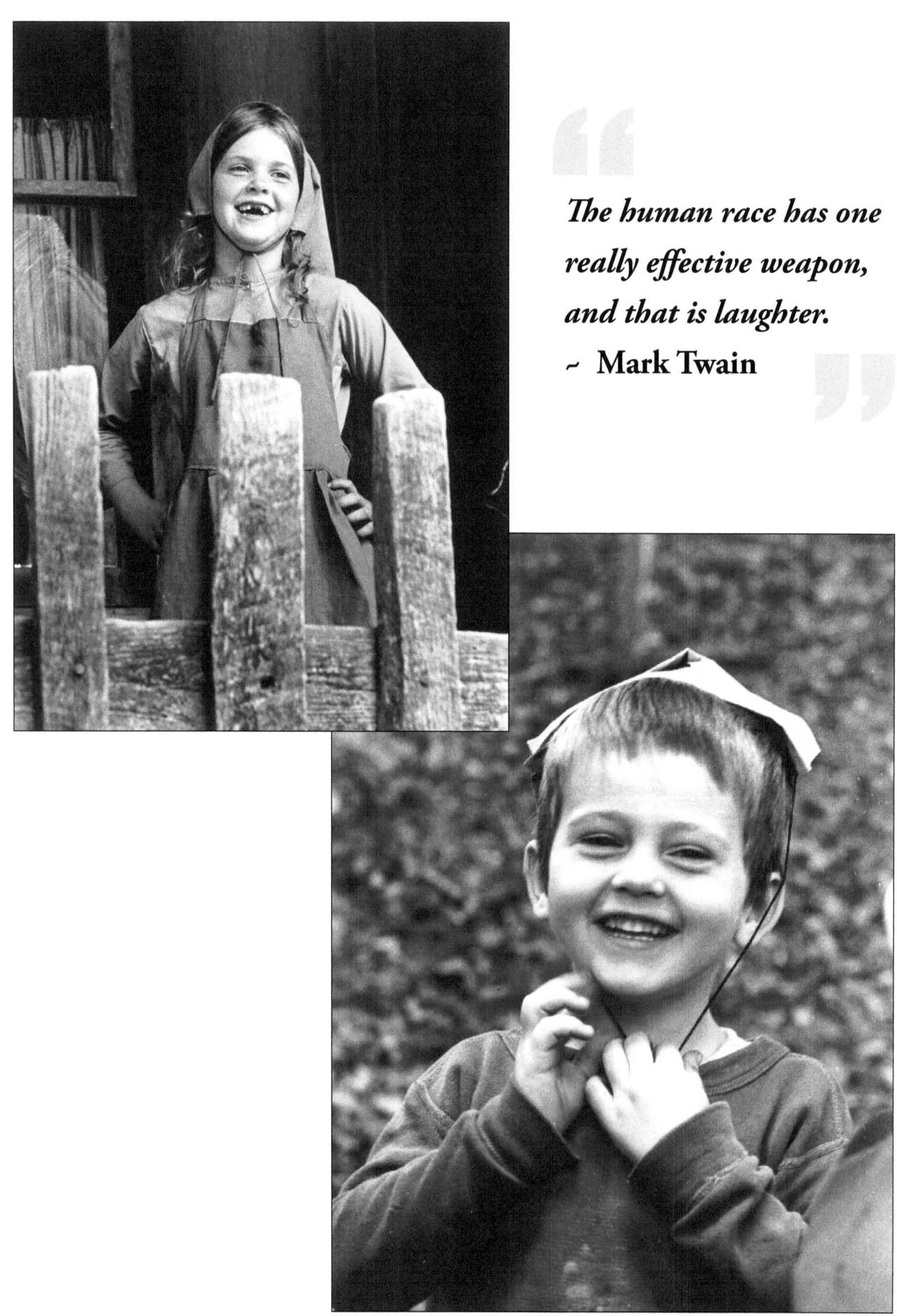

"
The human race has one really effective weapon, and that is laughter.
~ **Mark Twain**
"

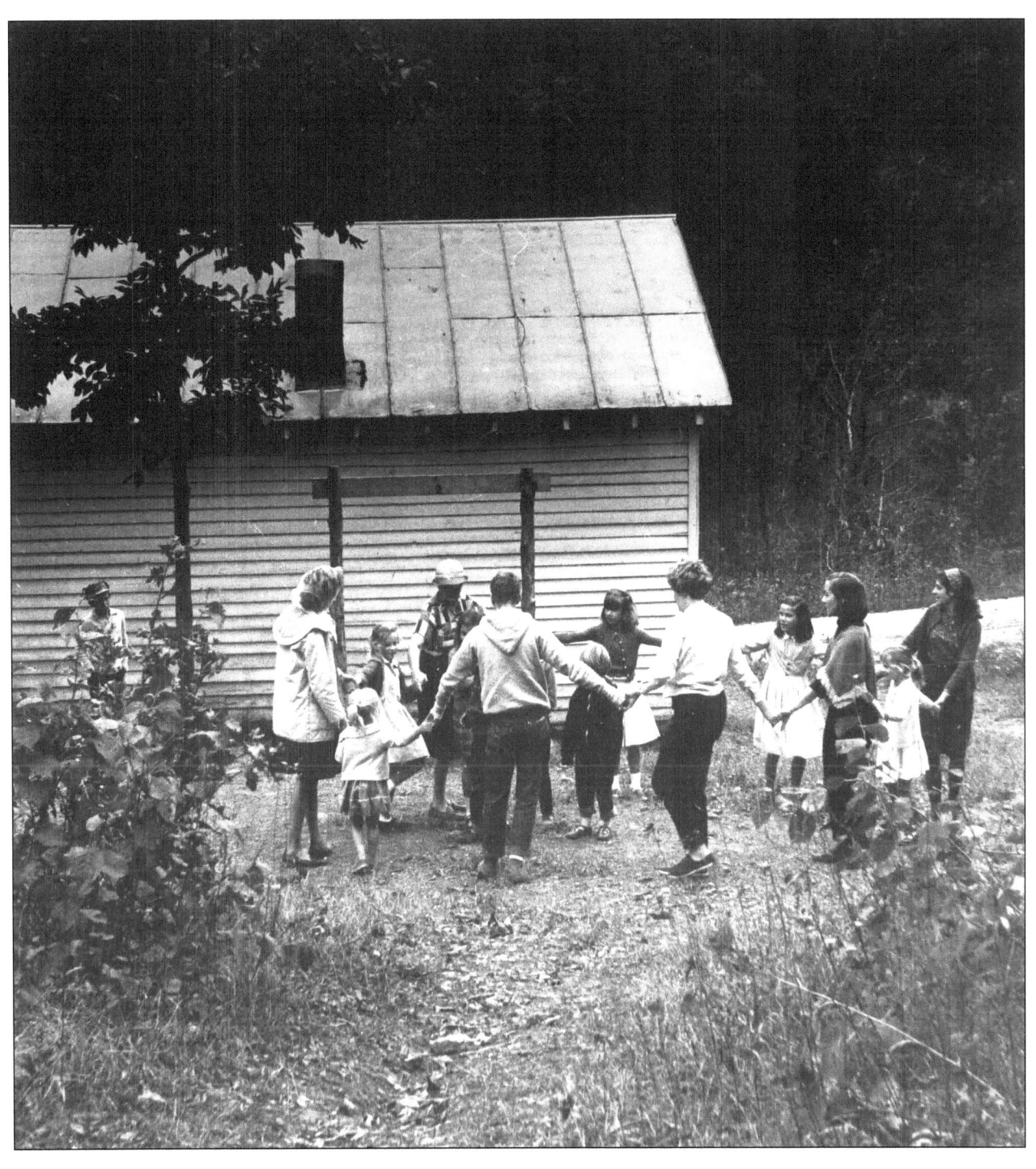

" *To watch us dance is to hear our hearts speak.* "
~Hopi Indian Saying

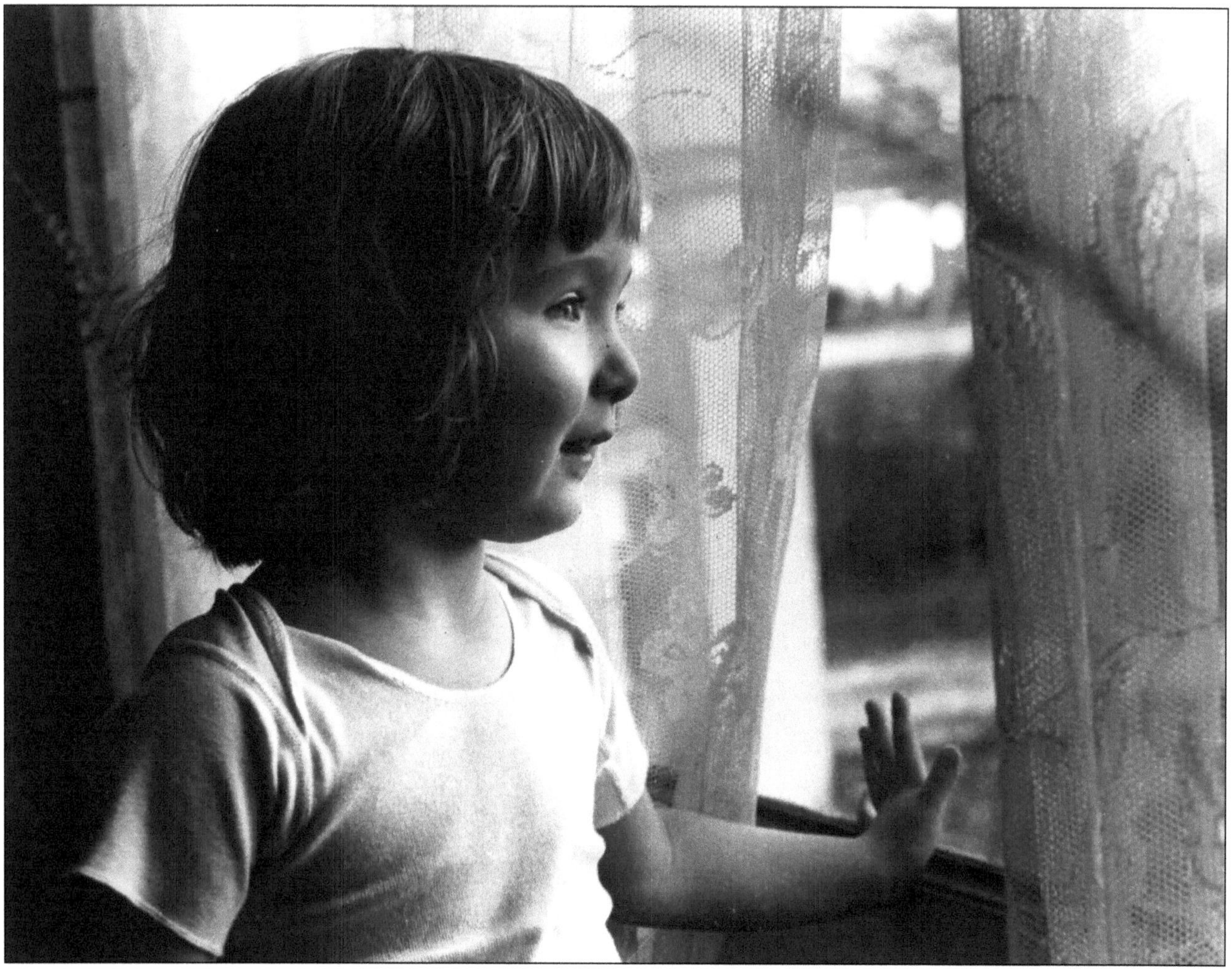

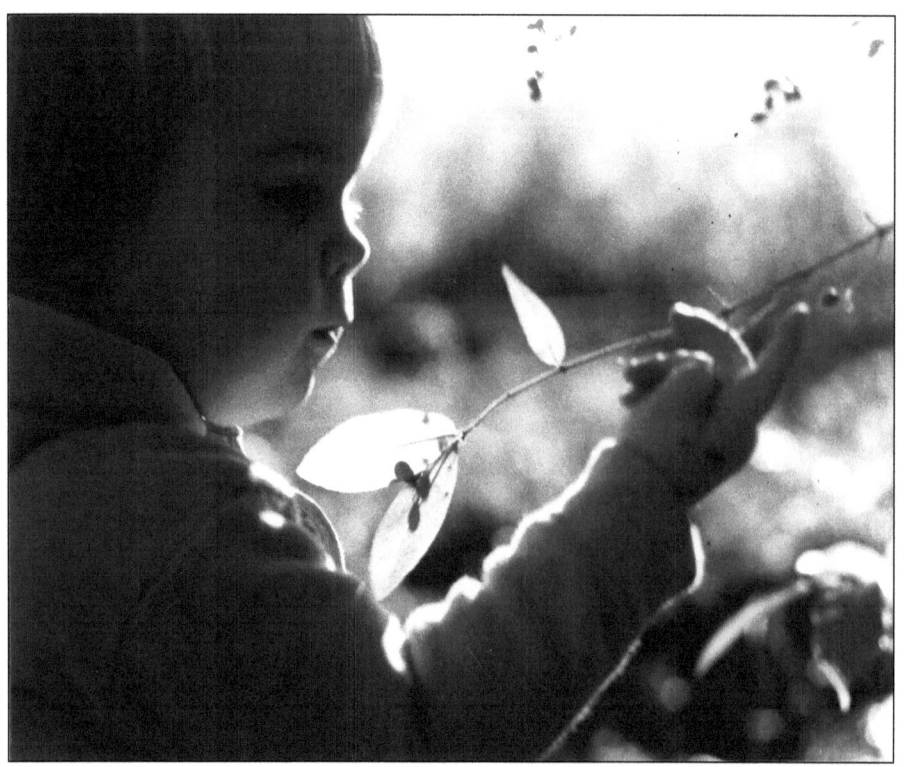

A sense of curiosity is nature's original school of education.
~Smiley Blanton

There are perhaps no days of our childhood we lived so fully as those we spent with a favorite book. ~ Marcel Proust

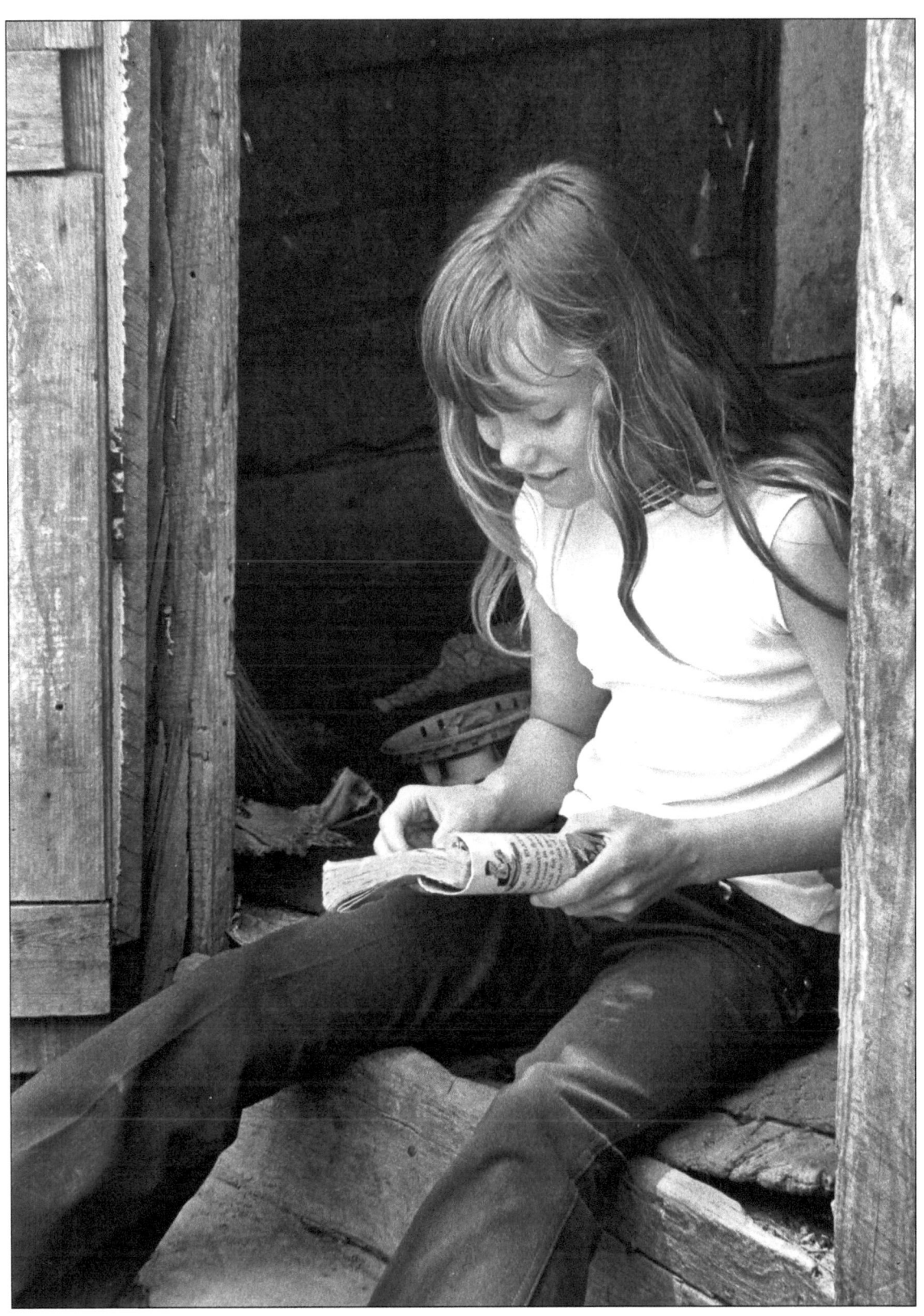

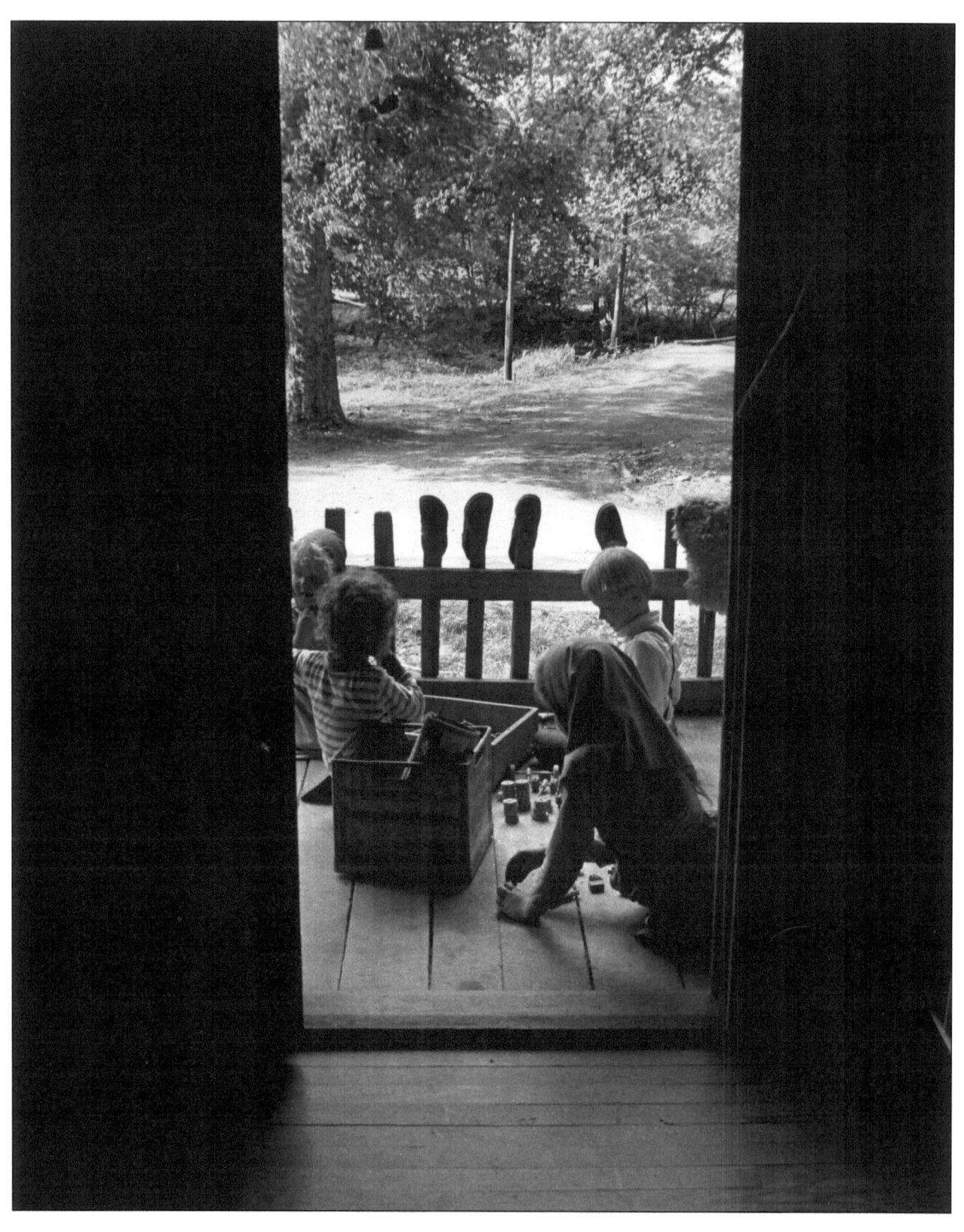

It is a happy talent to know how to play.
~ Ralph Waldo Emerson

*The philosophy of the school room
in one generation will be the philosophy
of government in the next.*
~ Abraham Lincoln

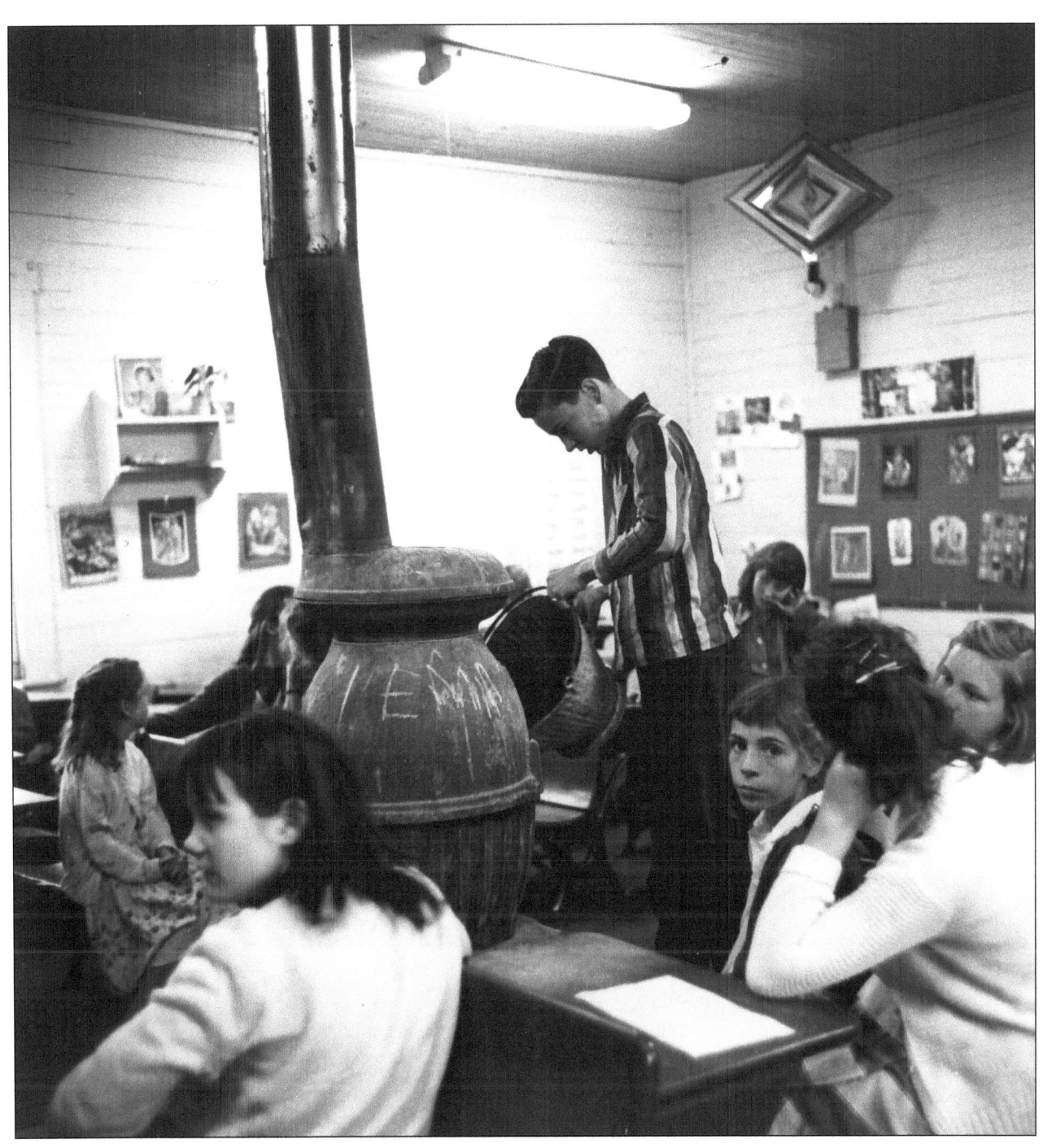

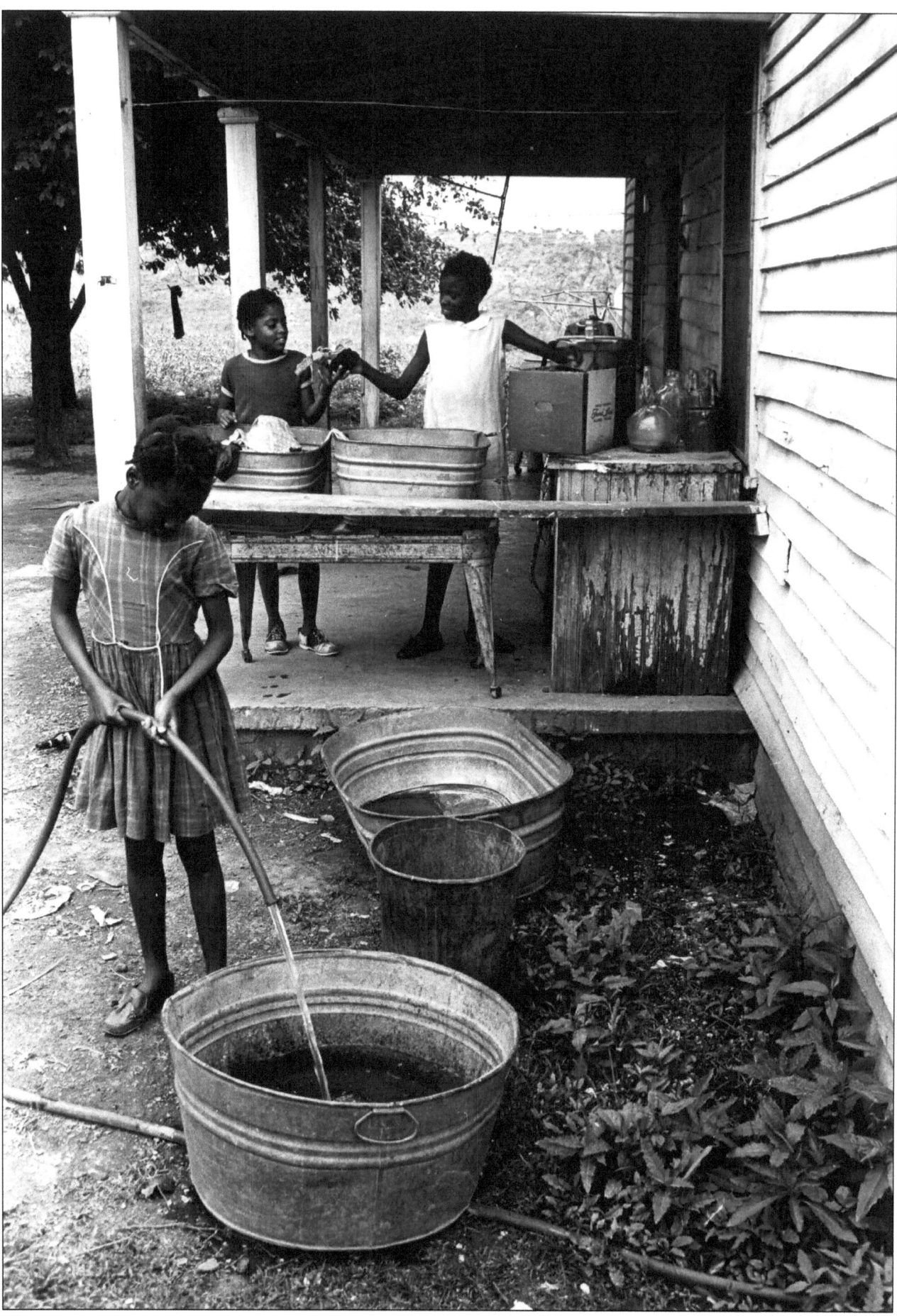

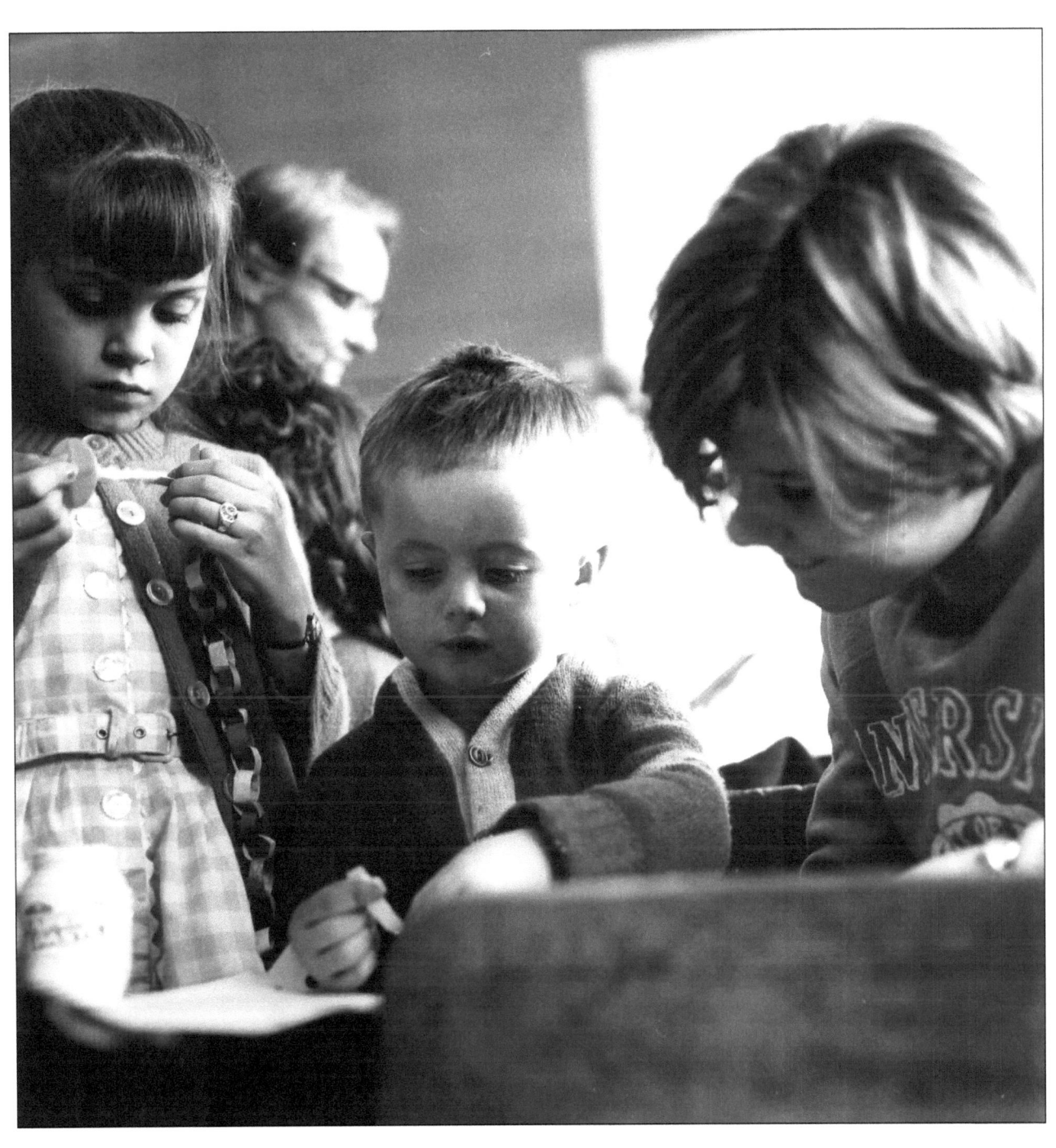

"

It is the supreme art of the teacher
to awaken joy in creative expression
and knowledge. ~ Albert Einstein

"

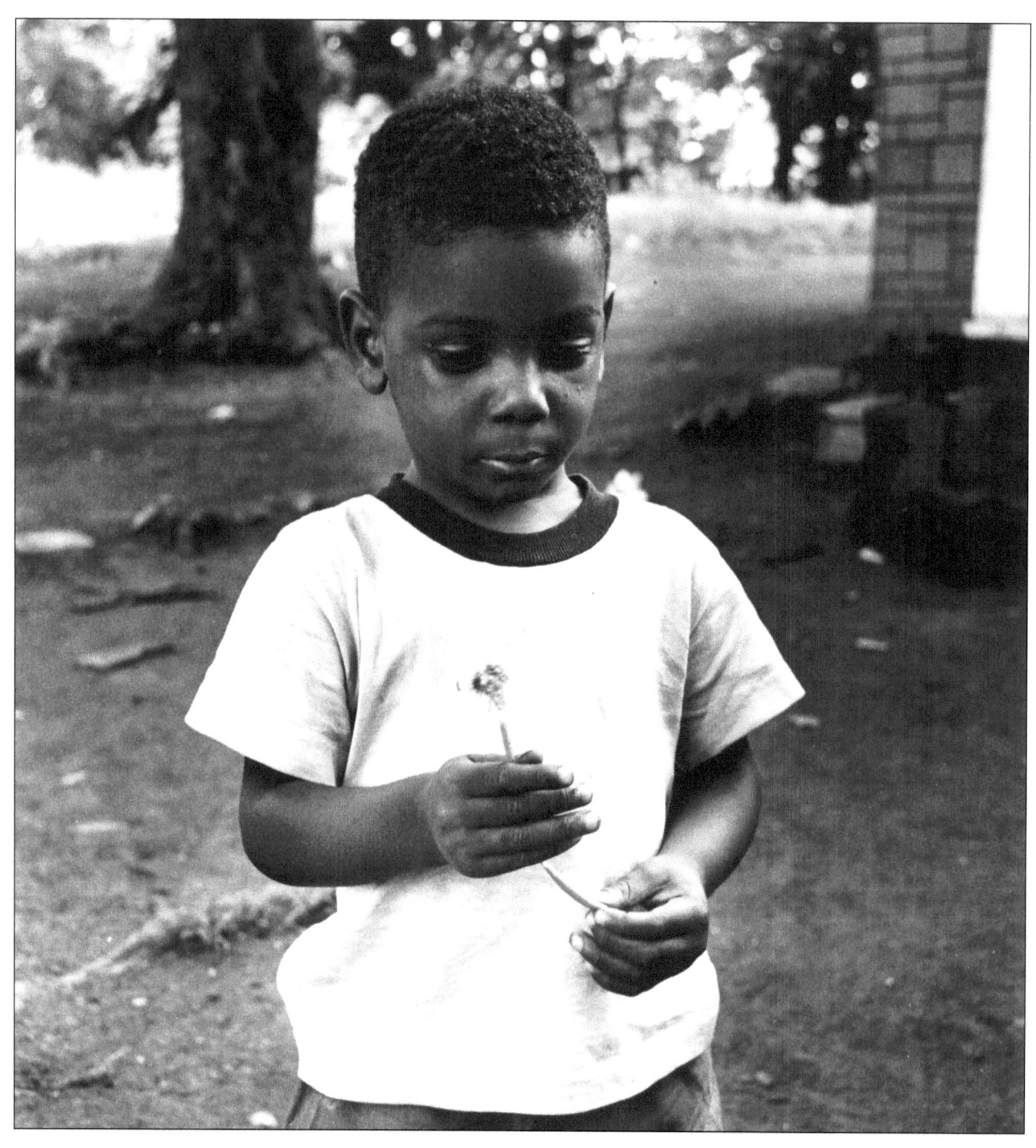

A rose can say "I love you",
orchids can enthrall,
but a weed bouquet
in a chubby fist,
yes, that says it all.
~Author Unknown

Nature will bear the closest inspection.
She invites us to lay our eye level with
her smallest leaf, and take an insect view
of its plain. ~ Henry David Thoreau

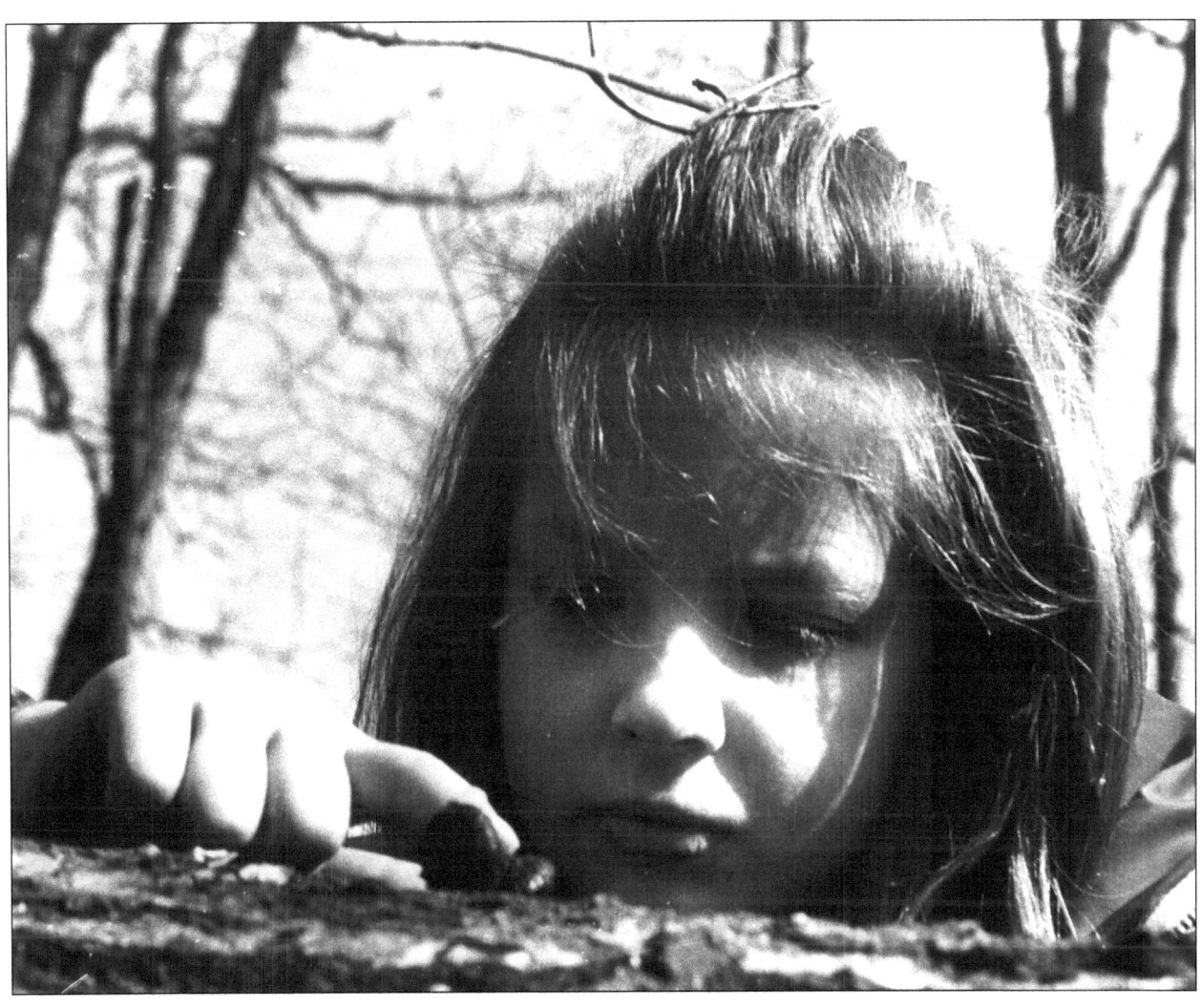

We are all travellers in the wilderness
of this world, and the best we can find
in our travels is an honest friend.
~ Robert Louis Stevenson

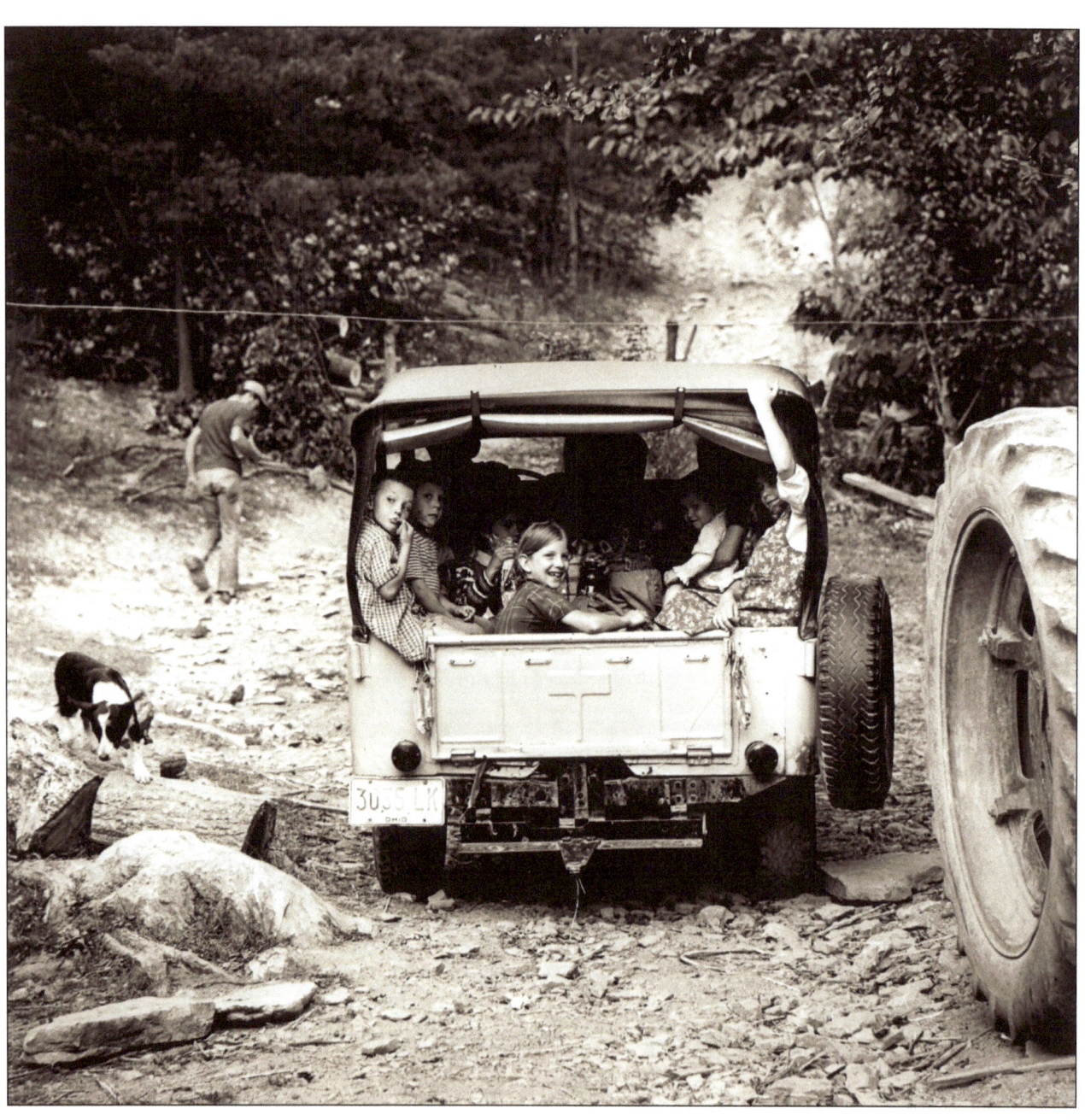

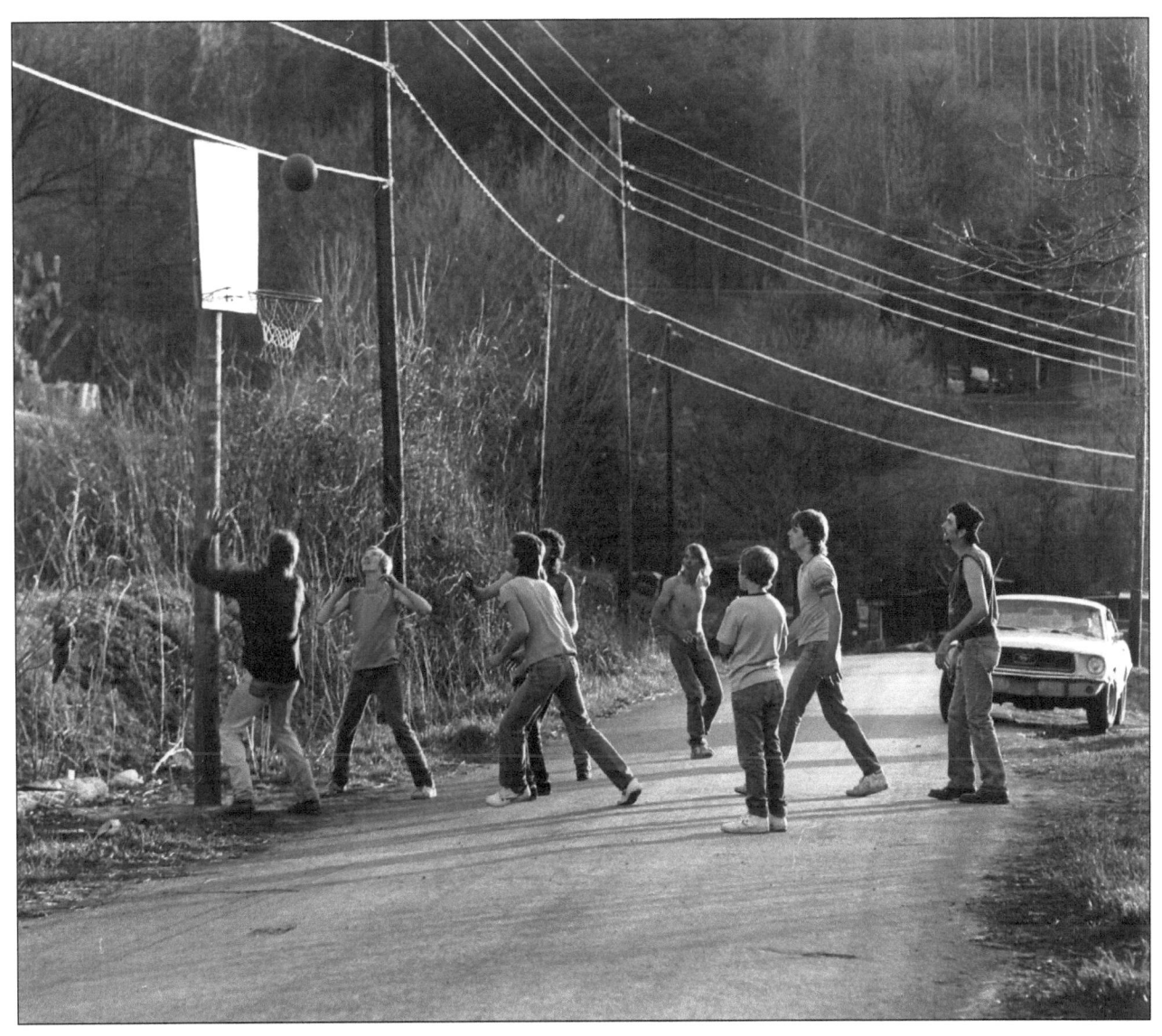

There are children playing in the streets who could solve some of my top problems in physics, because they have modes of sensory perception that I lost long ago. ~ J. Robert Oppenheimer

Youth smiles without any reason. It is one of its chiefest charms. ~ **Thomas Gray**

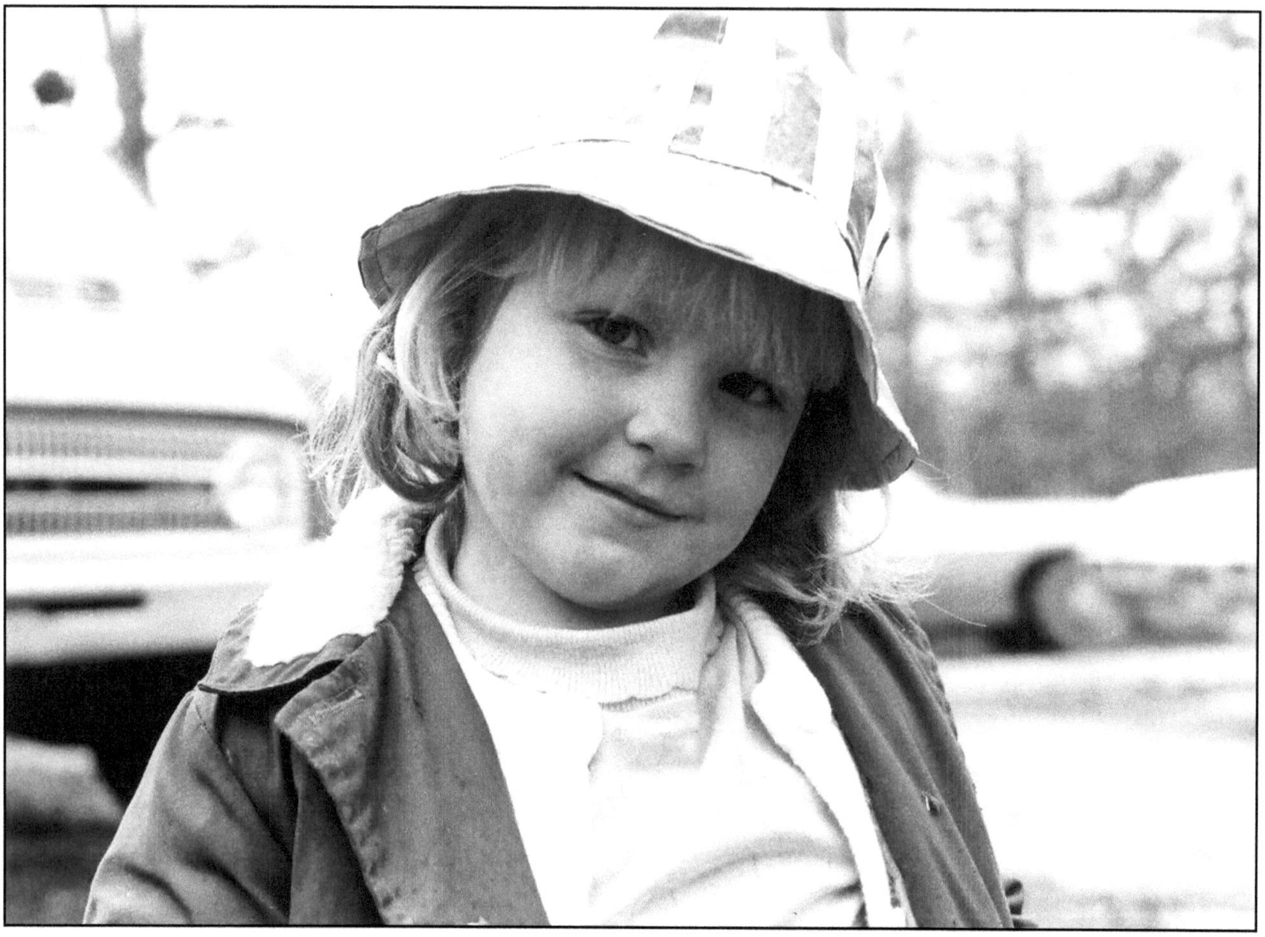

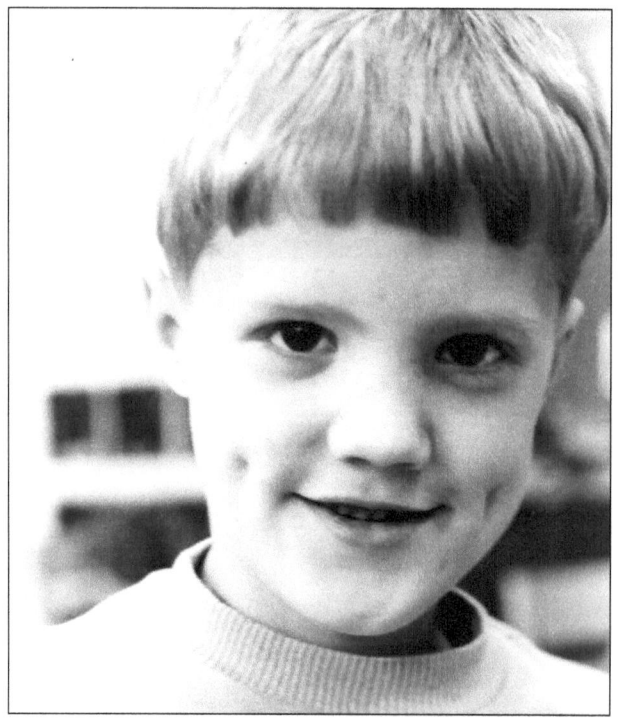

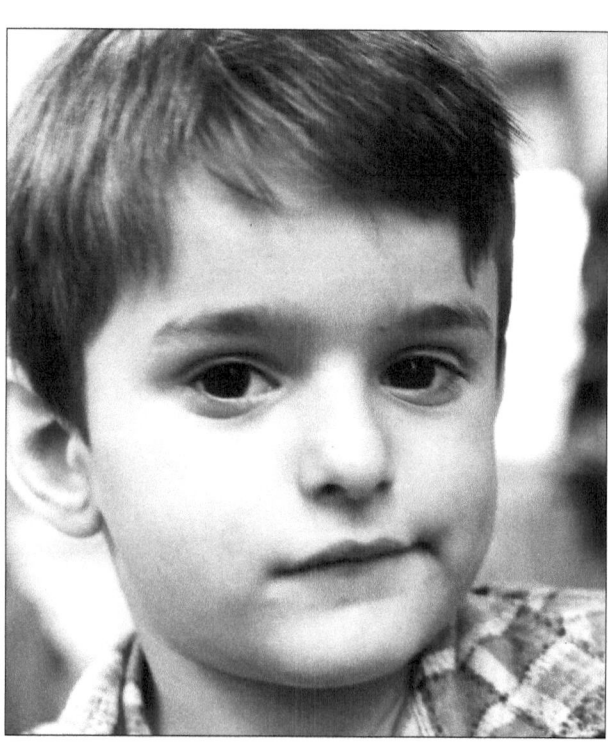

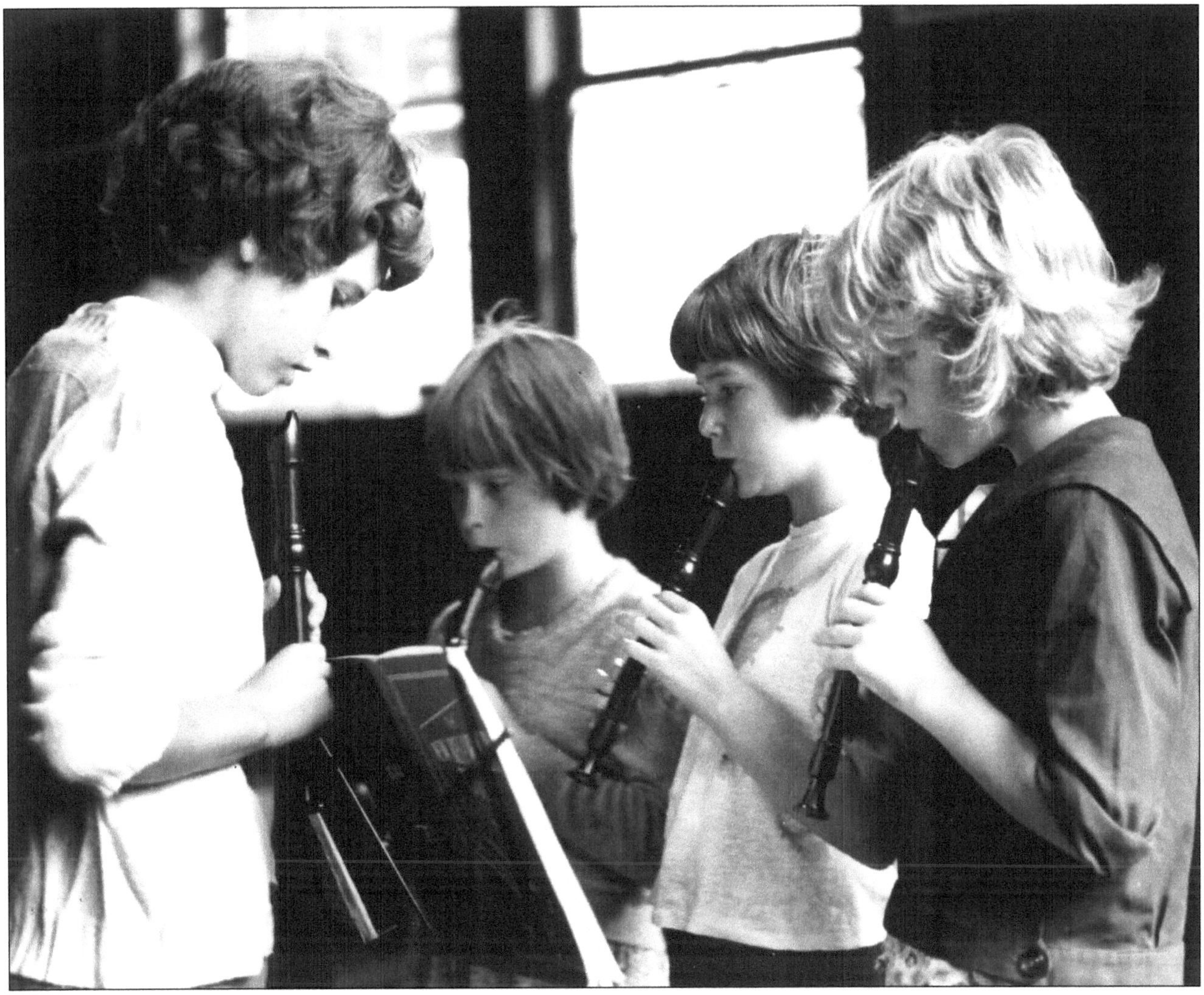

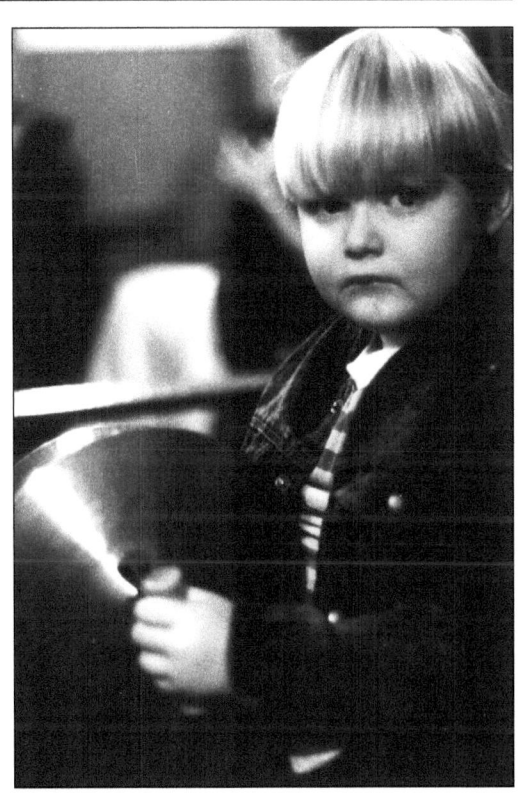

Music gives a soul to the universe, wings to the mind, flight to the imagination and life to everything. ~ **Plato**

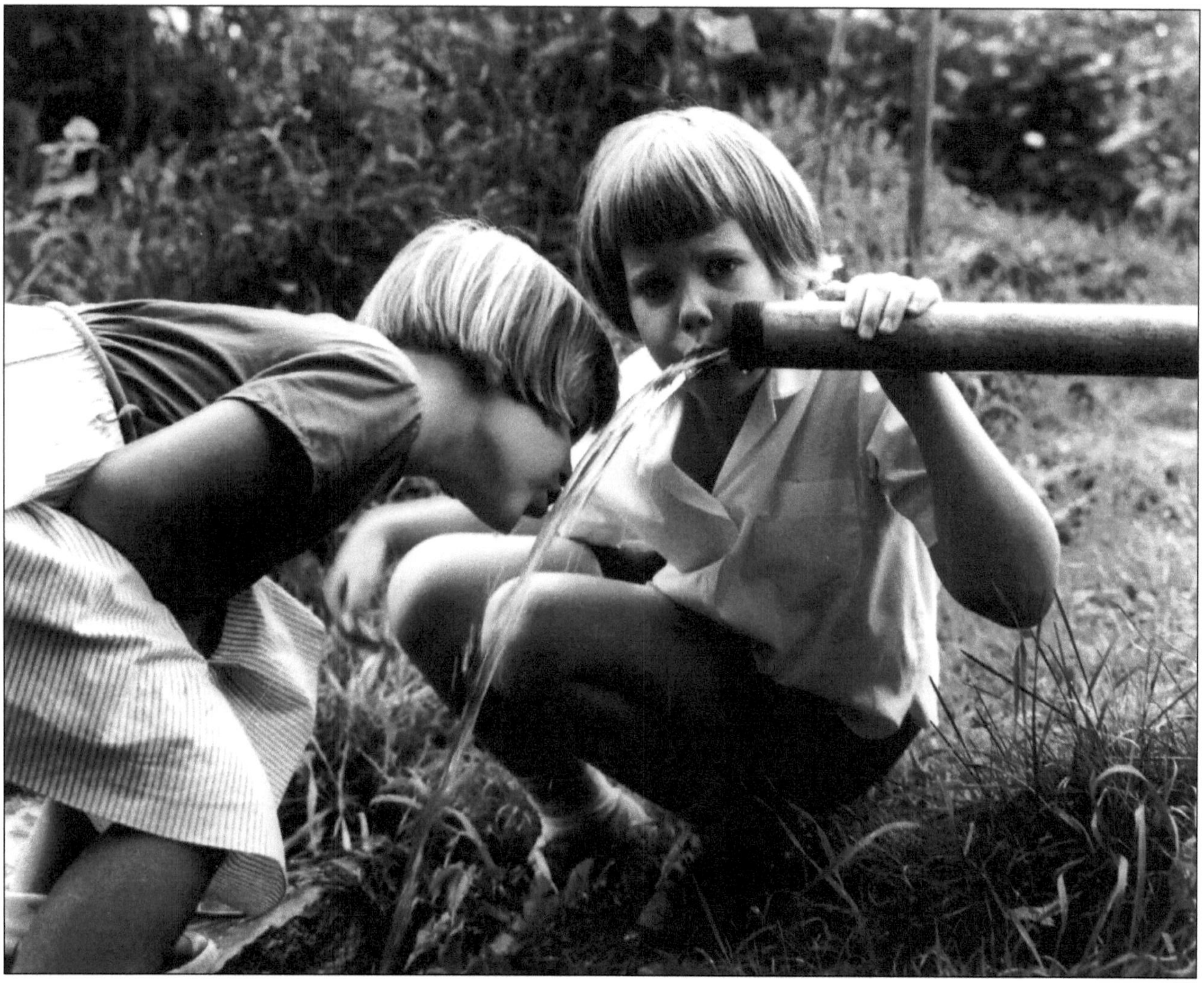

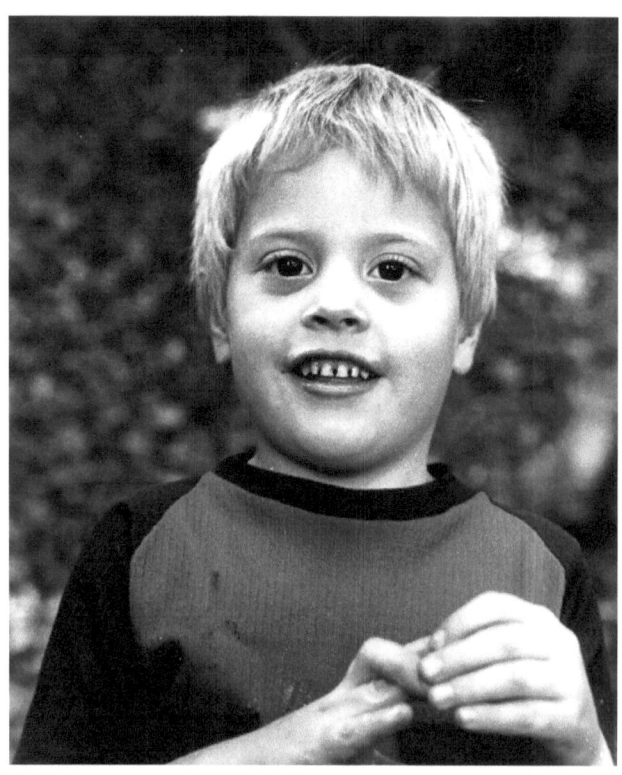
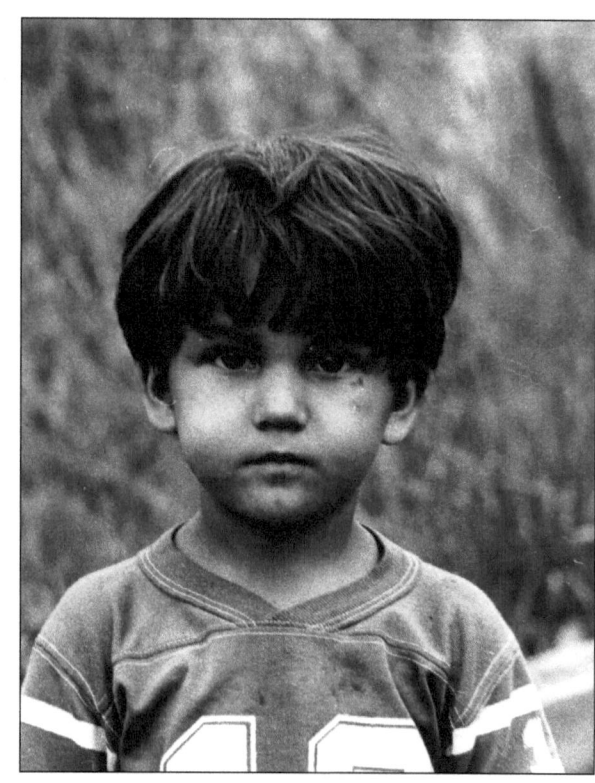

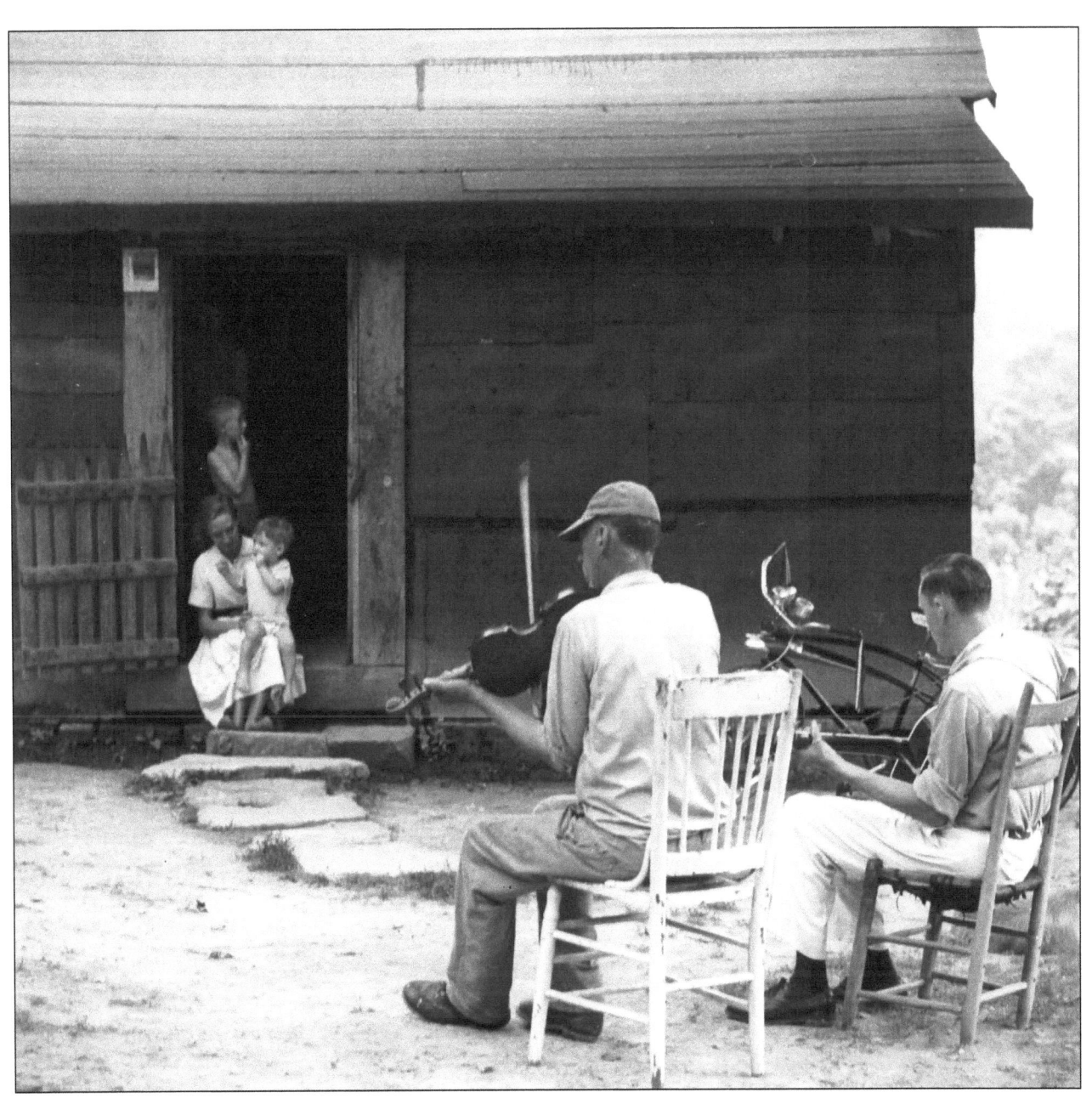

For the good are always the merry
Save by an evil chance
And the merry love the fiddle
And the merry love to dance.
~ William Butler Yeats

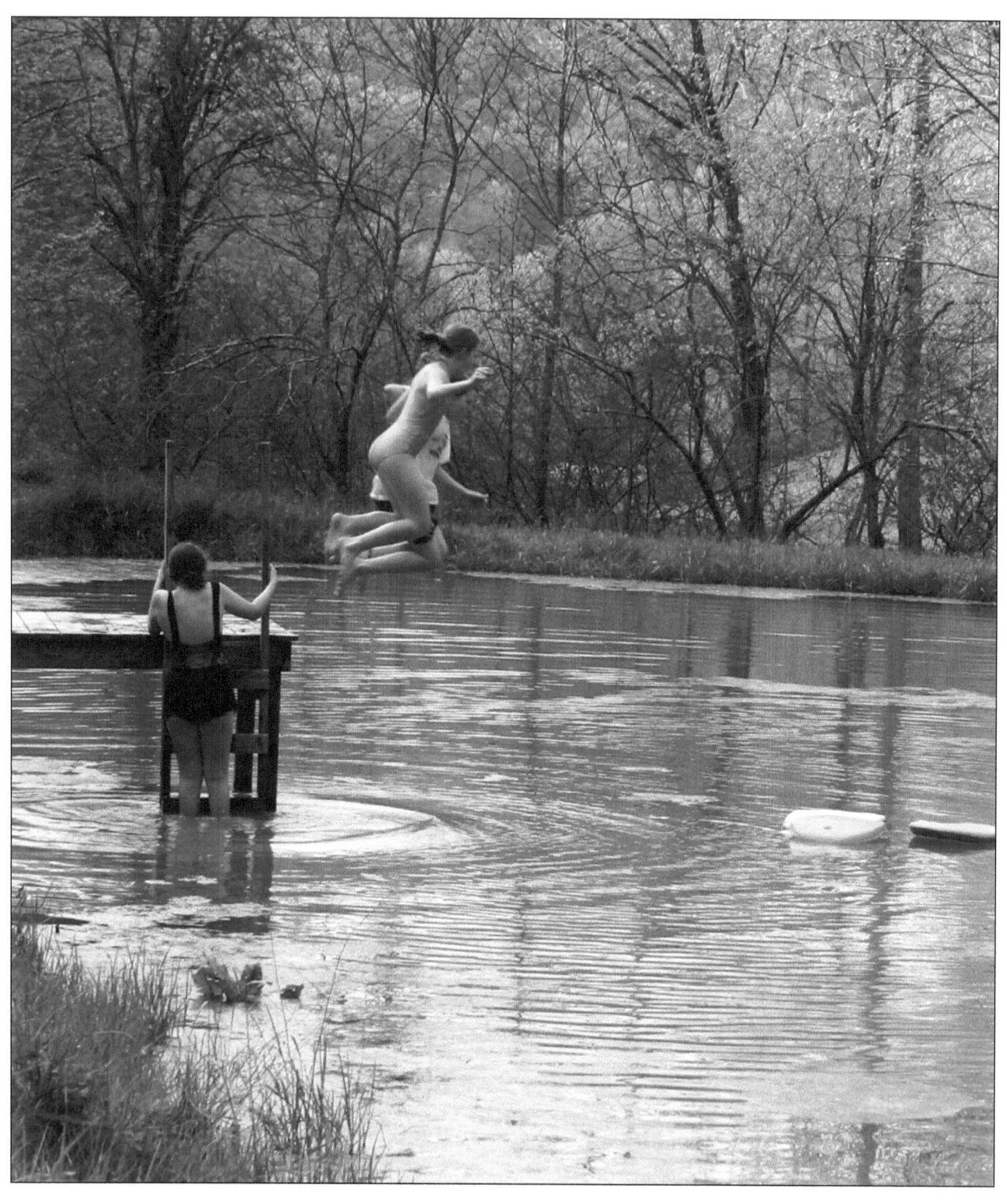

"The true object of all human life is play. Earth is a task garden; heaven is a playground. ~ G K Chesterton

We could never have loved the earth so well
if we had had no childhood in it. ~ George Eliot

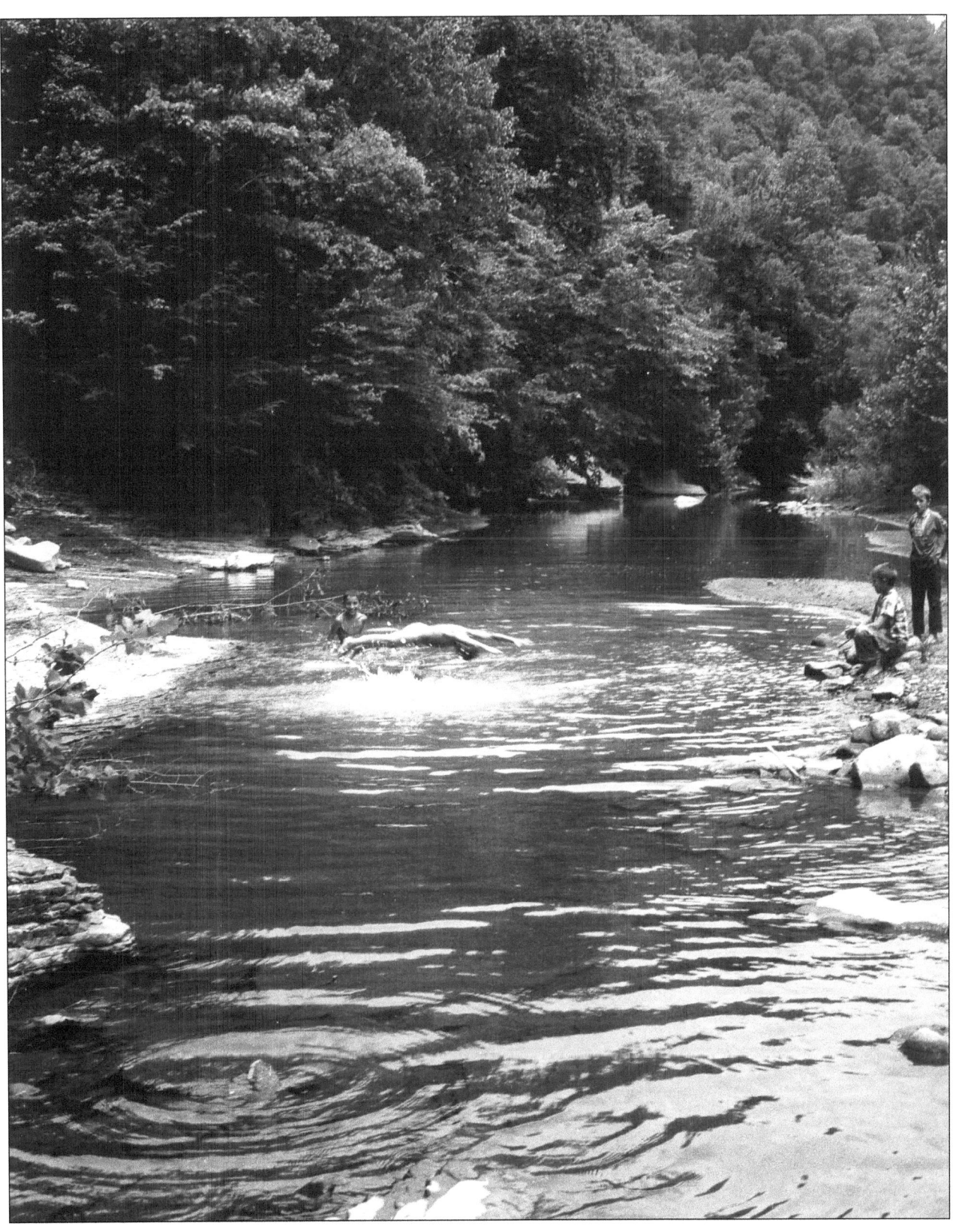

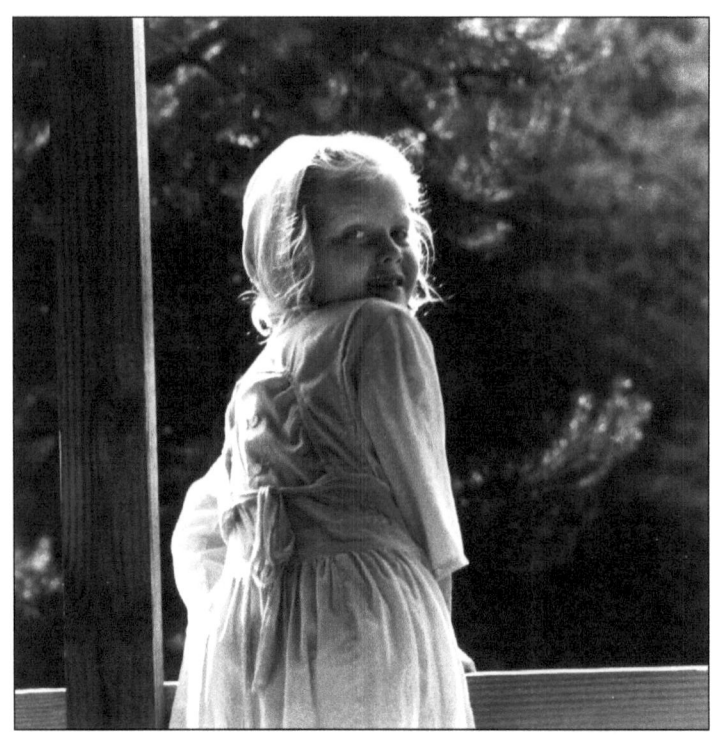

A kind heart is a fountain of gladness, making everything in its vicinity freshen into smiles.
~ **Washington Irving**

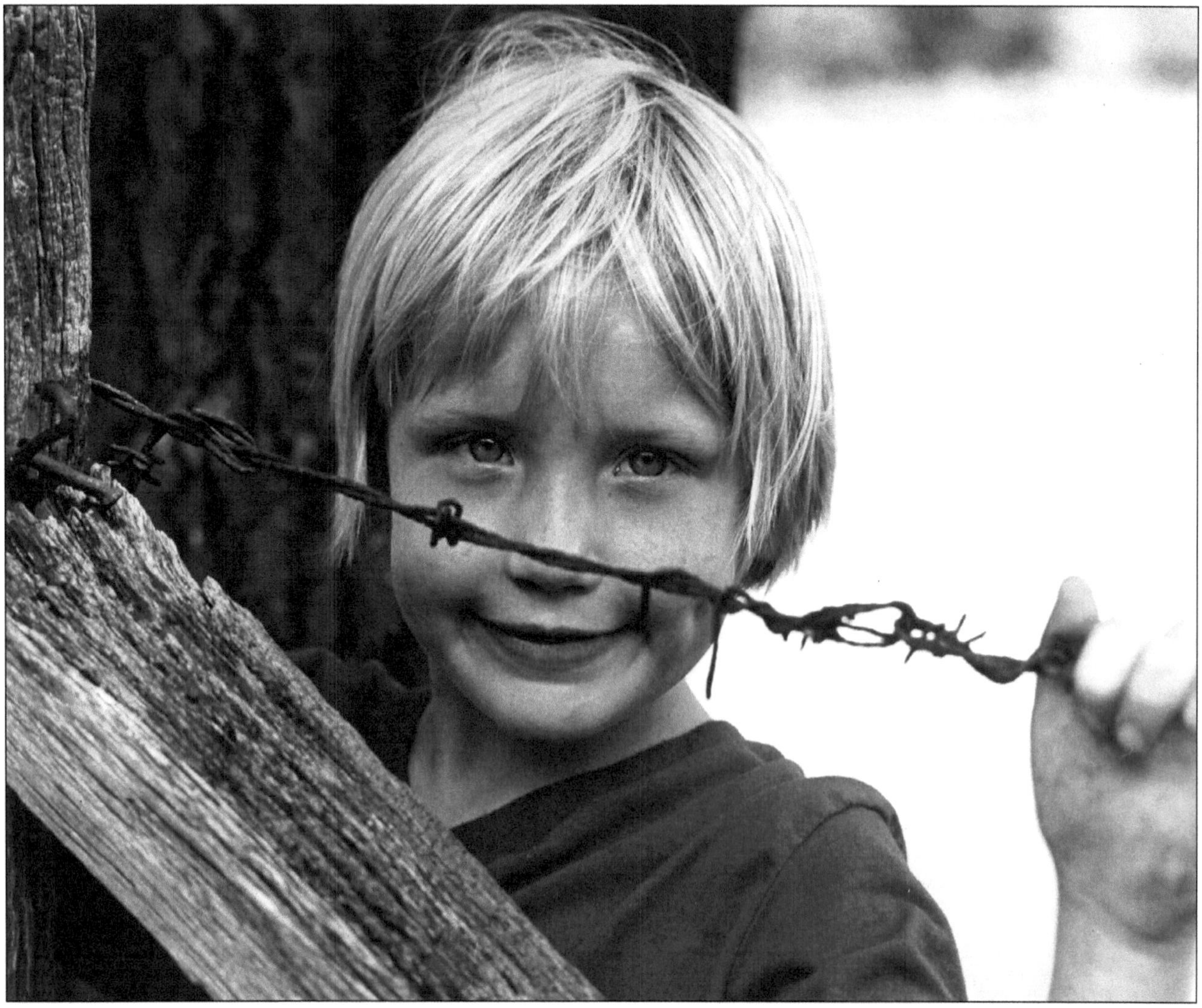

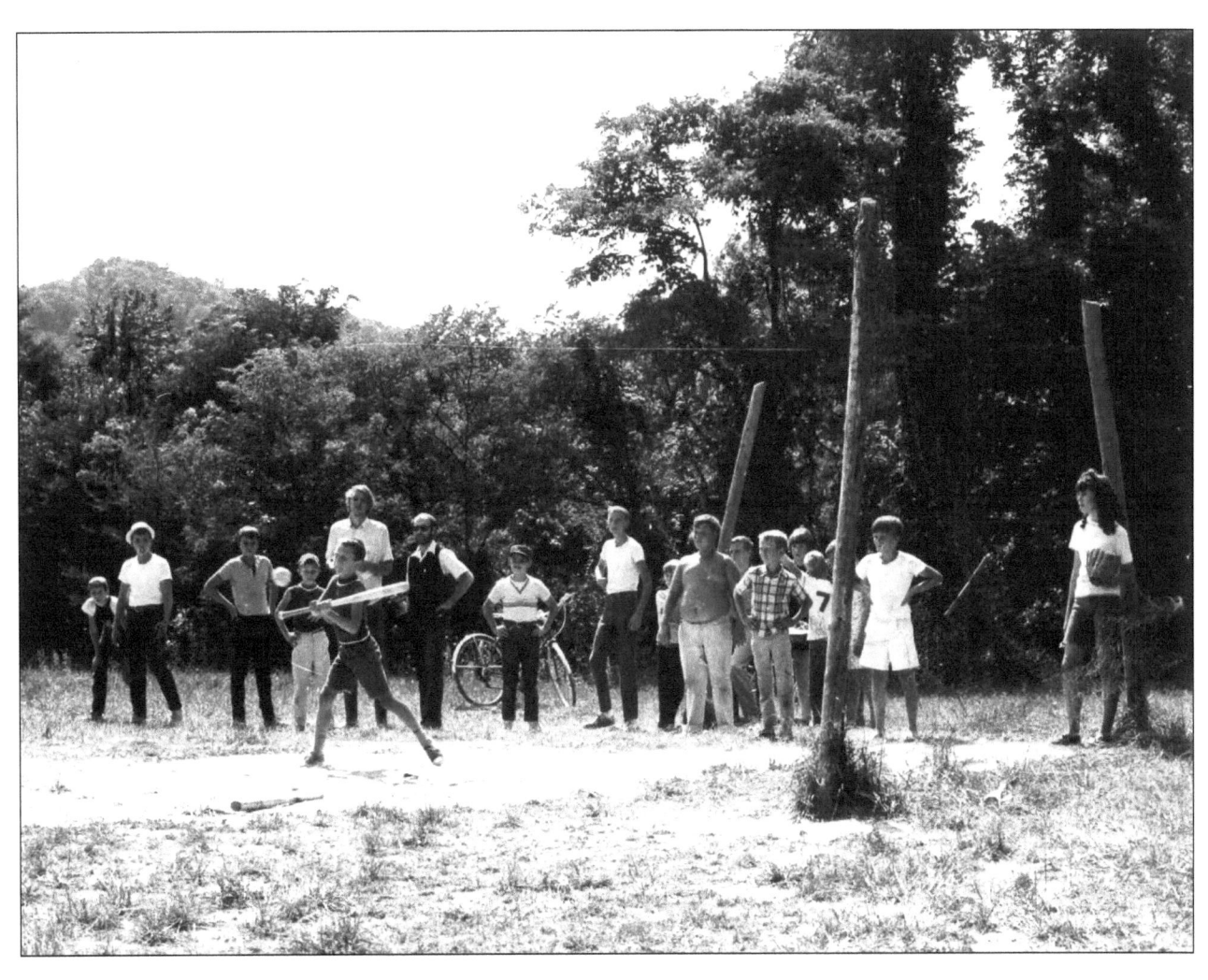

On the green they watched their sons
Playing till too dark to see,
As their fathers watched them once,
As my father once watched me.
~ Edmund Blunden

Rest is not idleness, and to lie sometimes on the grass under the trees on a summer's day, listening to the murmur of water, or watching the clouds float across the blue sky, is by no means waste of time. ~John Lubbock

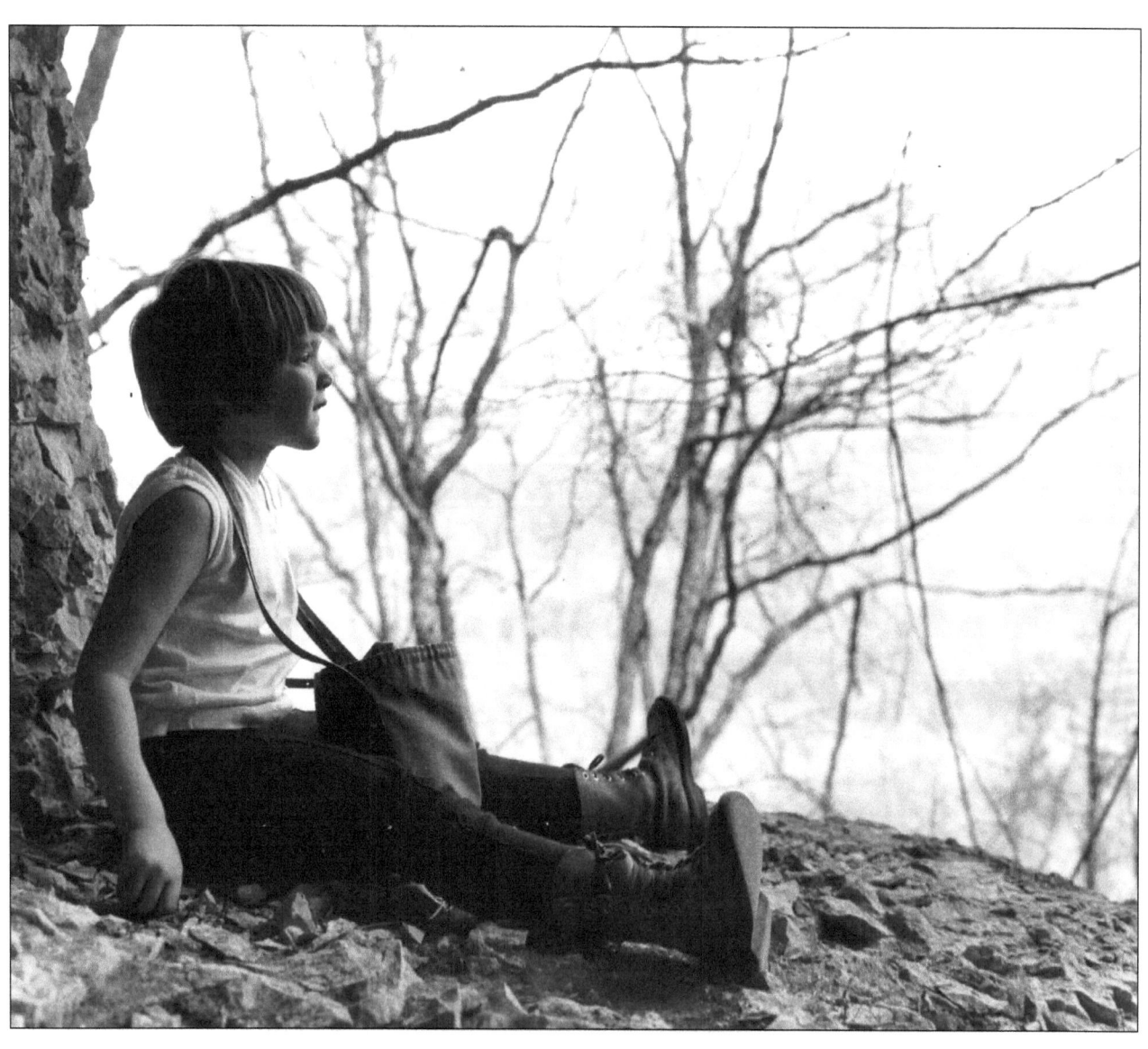

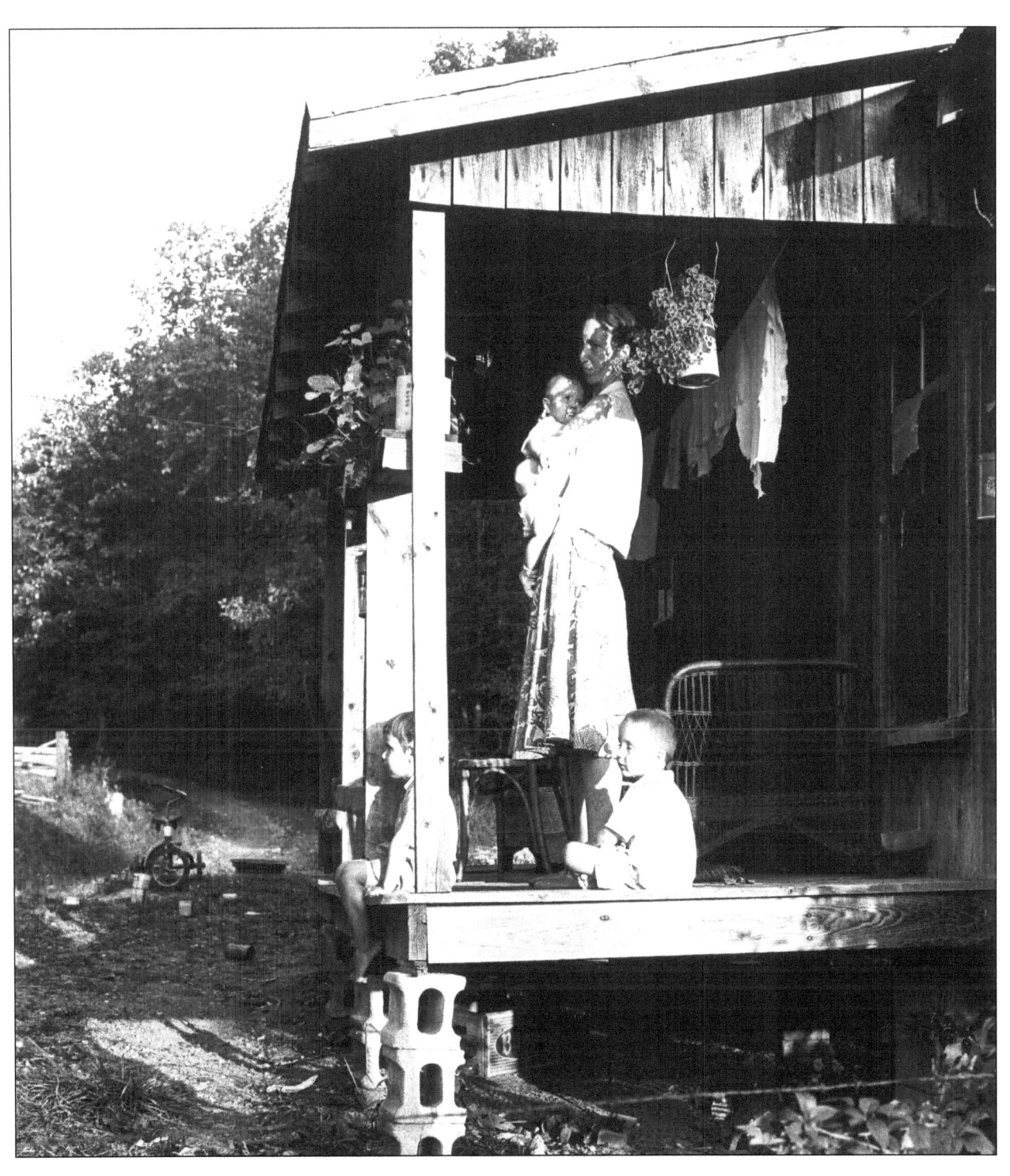

> *My mother had a great deal of trouble
> with me, but I think she enjoyed it.*
> ~ **Mark Twain**

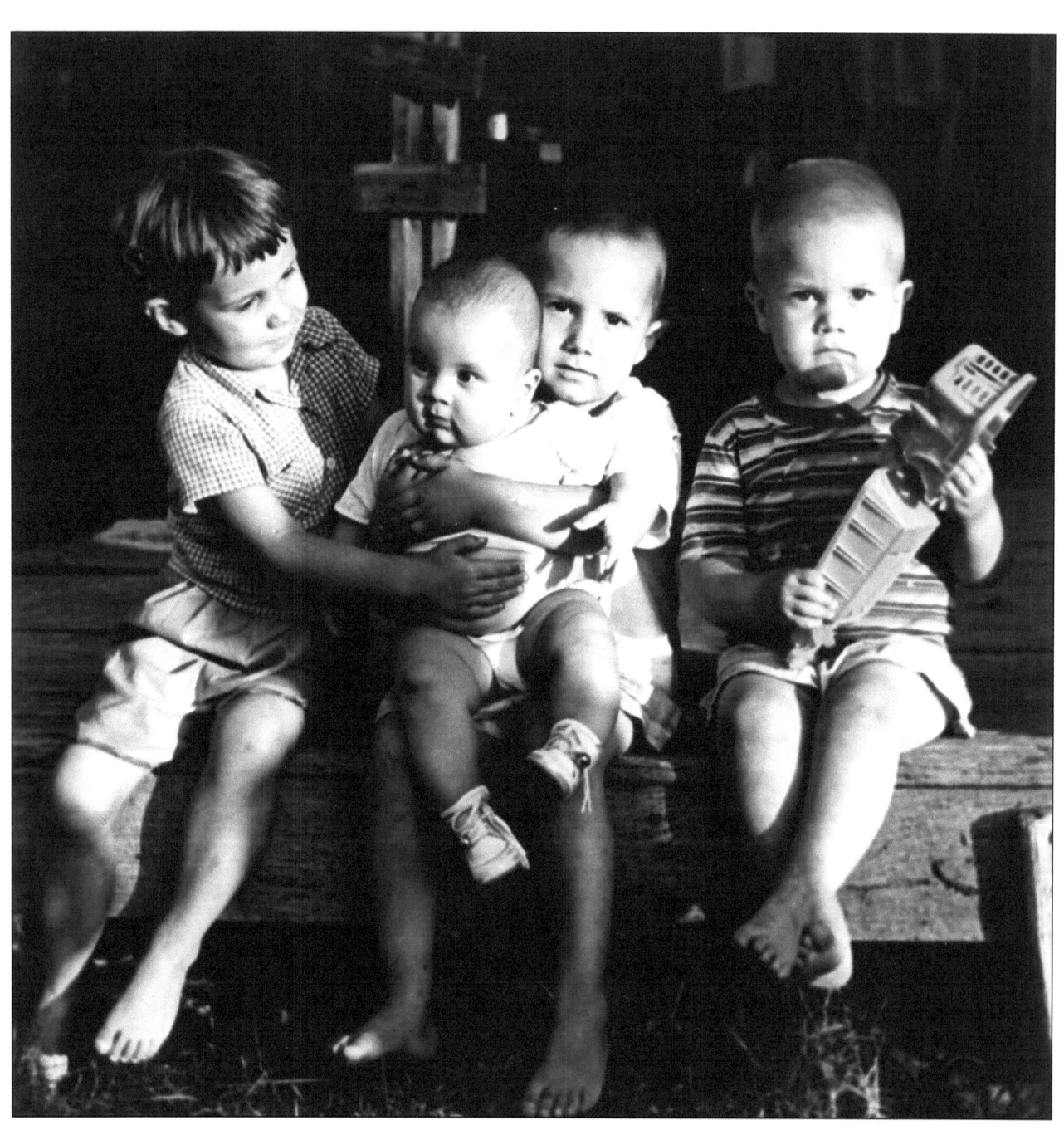

The happiest moments of my life have been the few which I have passed at home in the bosom of my family. ~ Thomas Jefferson

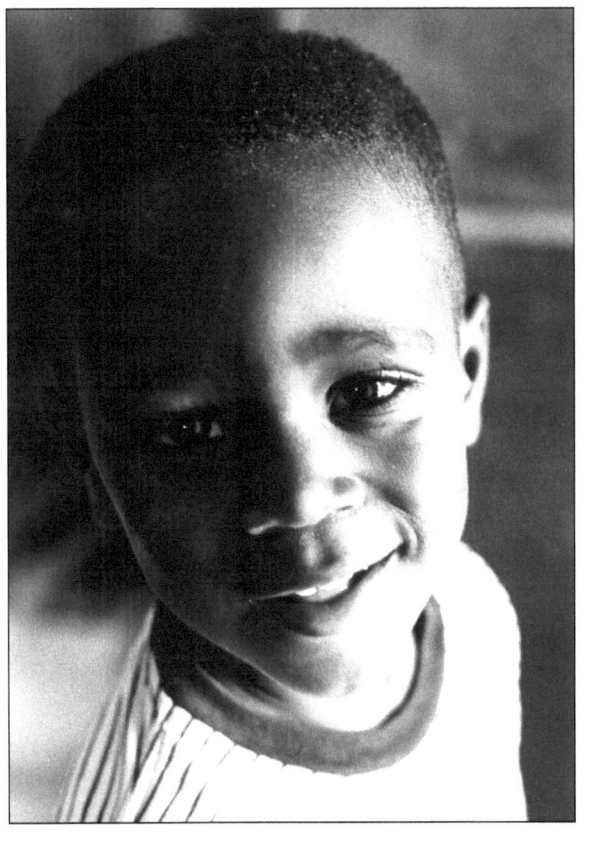

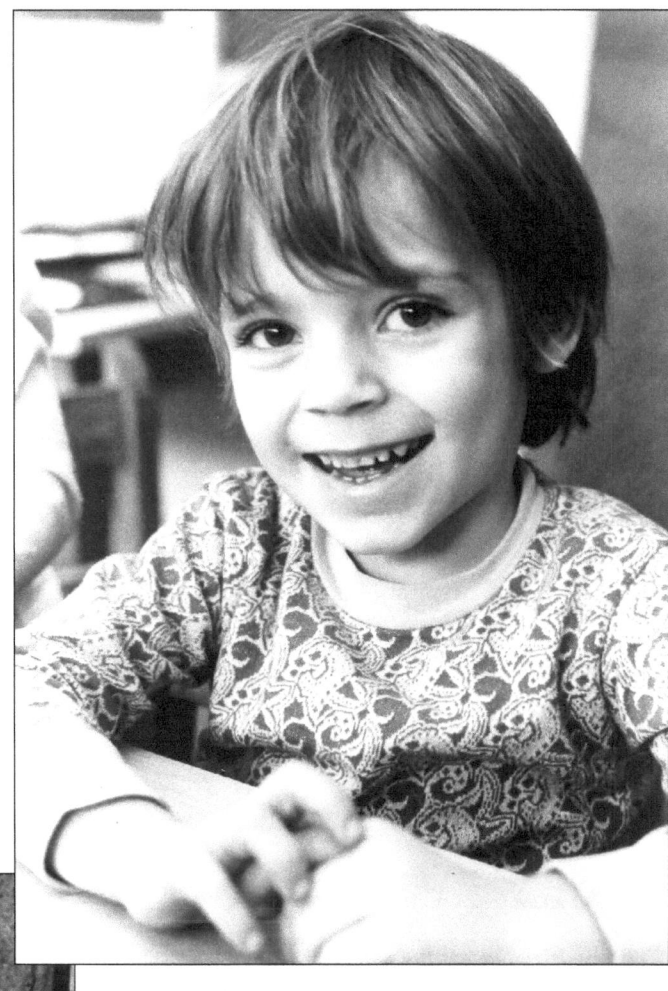

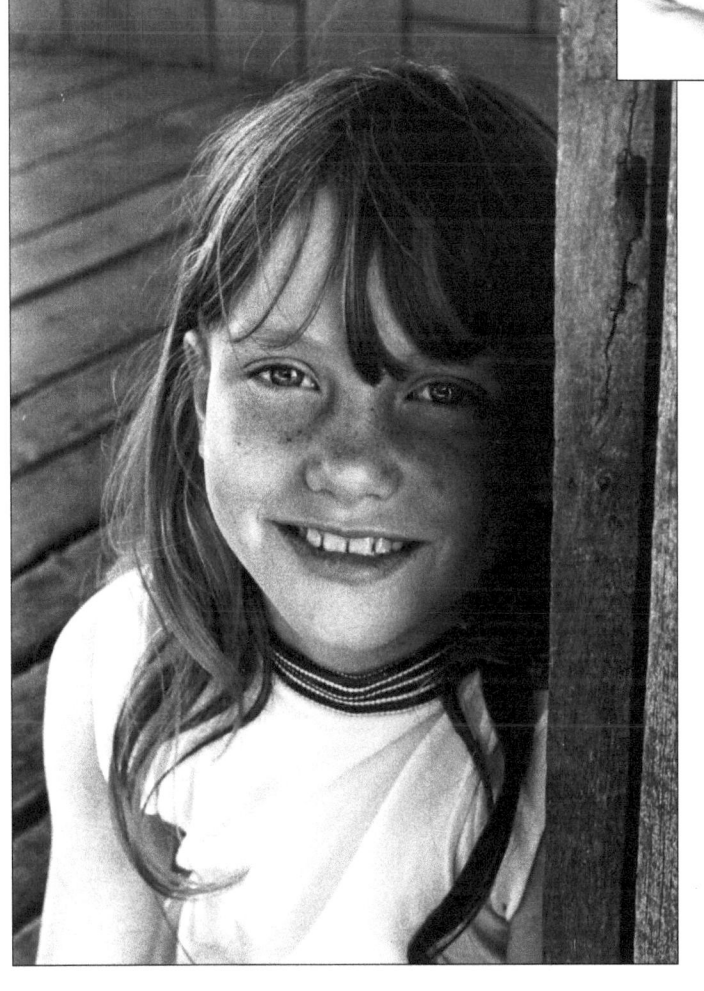

What sunshine is to flowers,
smiles are to humanity.
These are but trifles, to be
sure; but scattered along
life's pathway, the good they
do is inconceivable.
~ Joseph Addison

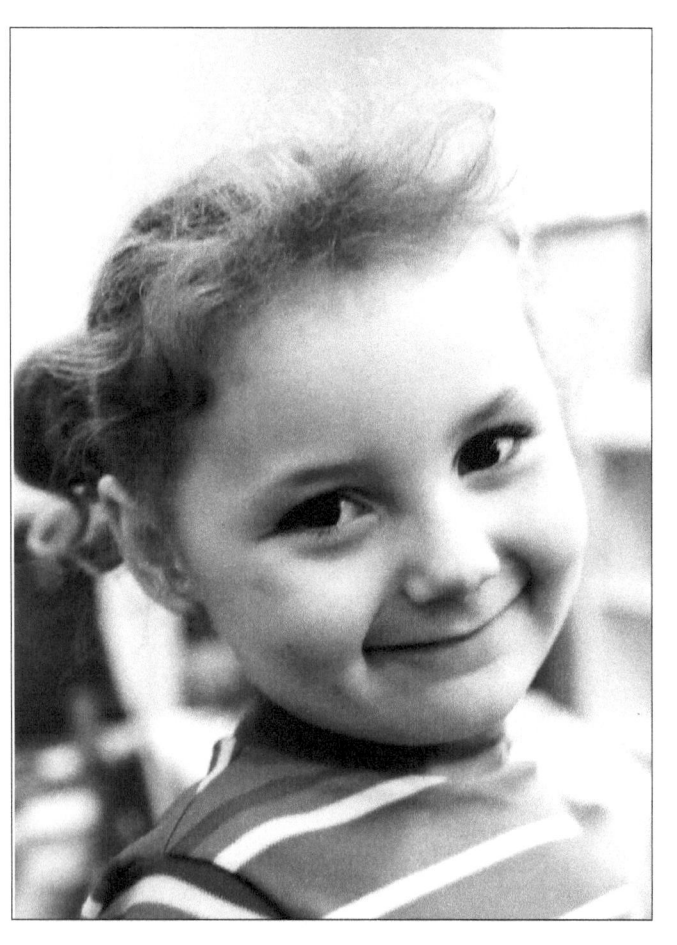

> *Every child comes with the message that God is not yet discouraged of man.*
> ~Rabindranath Tagore

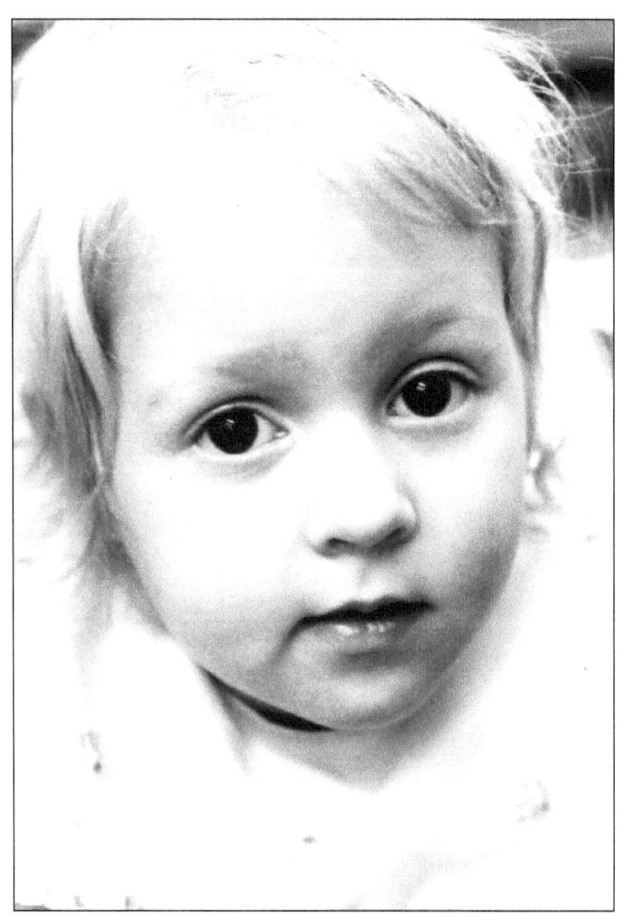

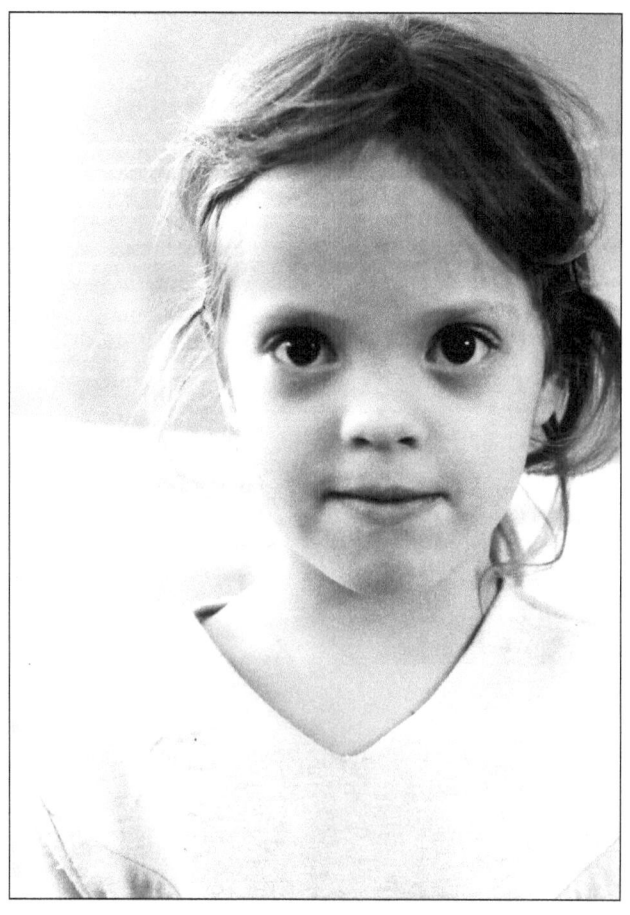

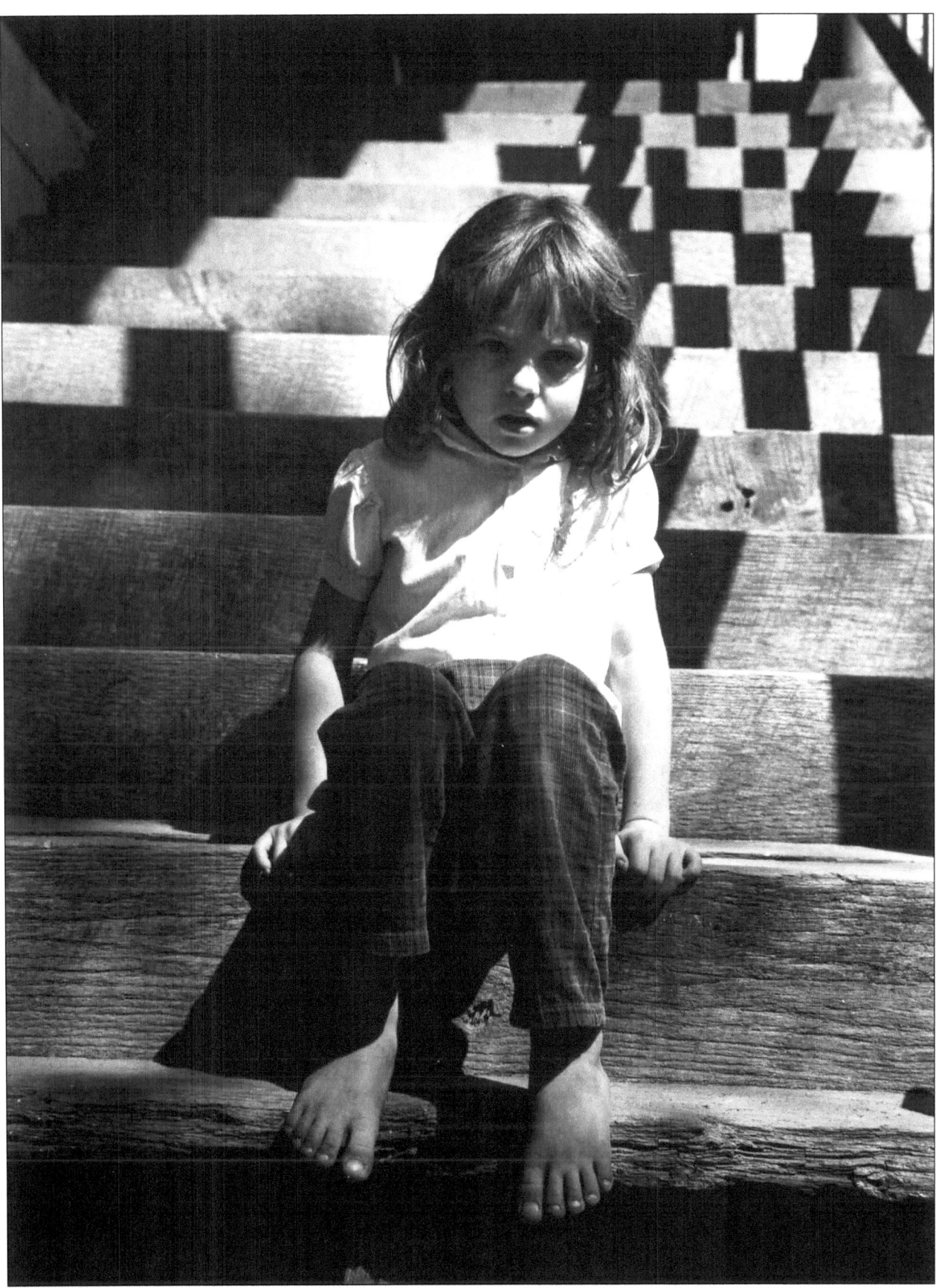

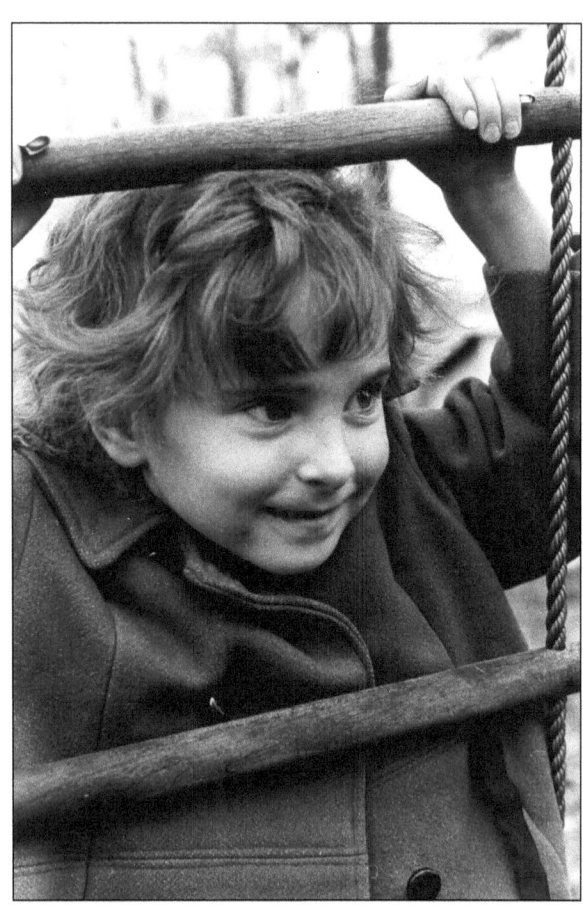
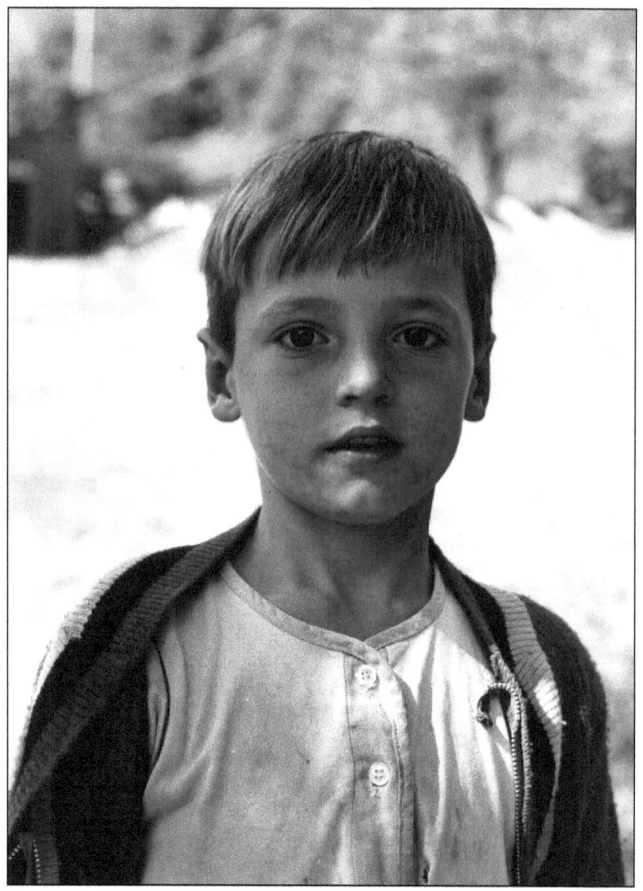

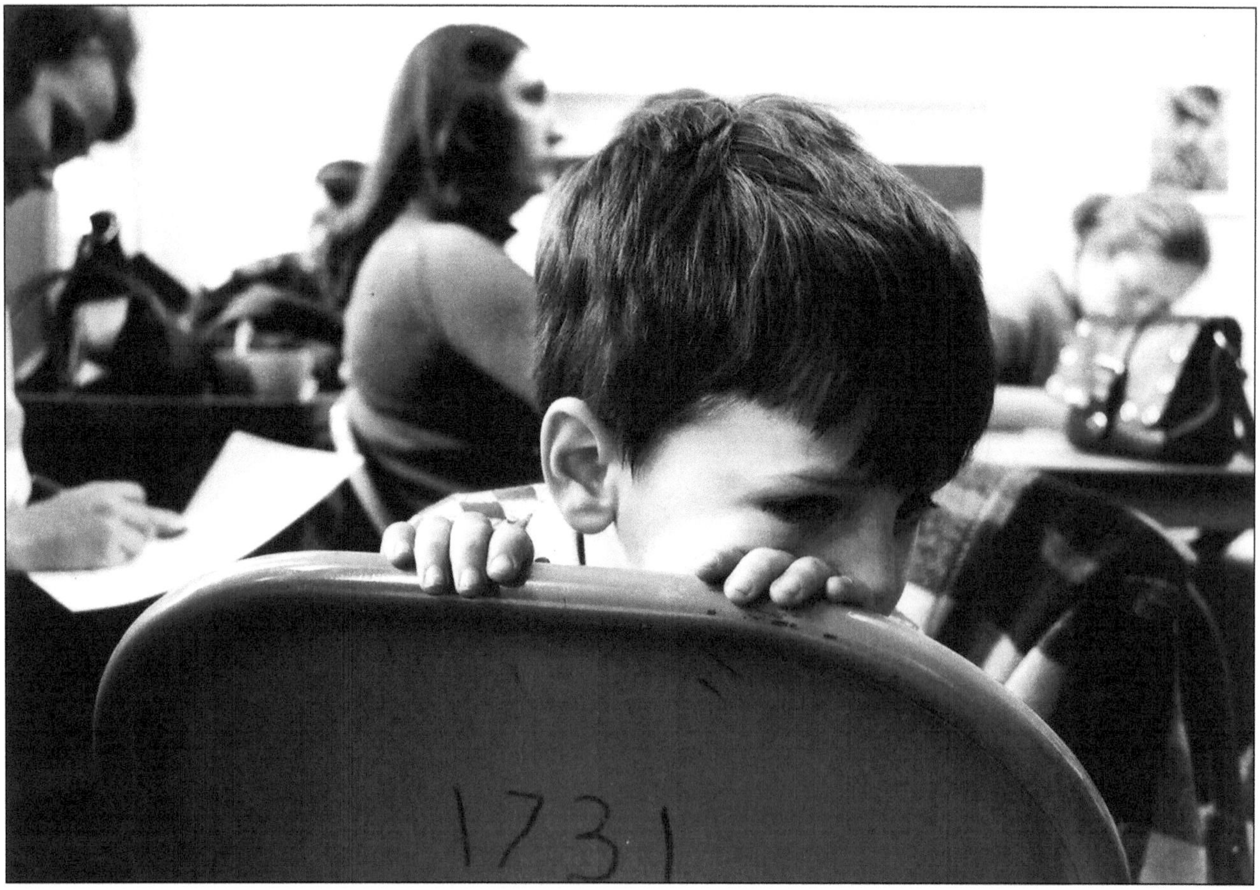

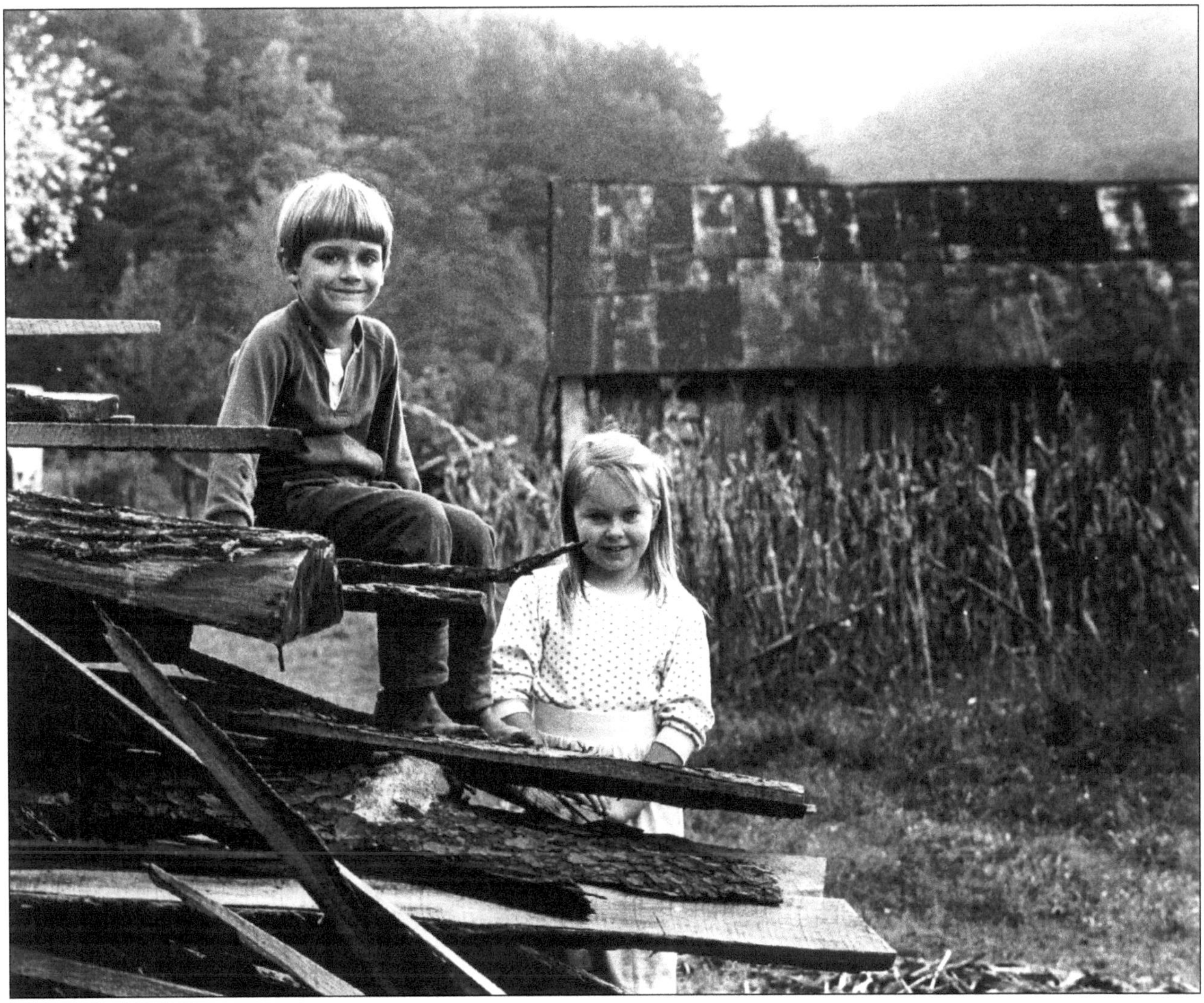

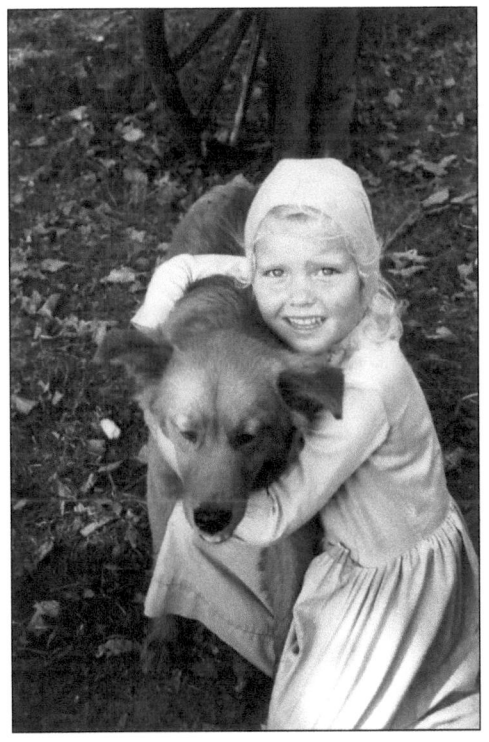

*You don't choose your family.
They are God's gift to you, as
you are to them.*
~ **Desmond Tutu**

As you sit on the hillside, or lie prone under the trees of the forest, or sprawl wet-legged by a mountain stream, the great door, that does not look like a door, opens.
~ Stephen Graham, *The Gentle Art of Tramping.*

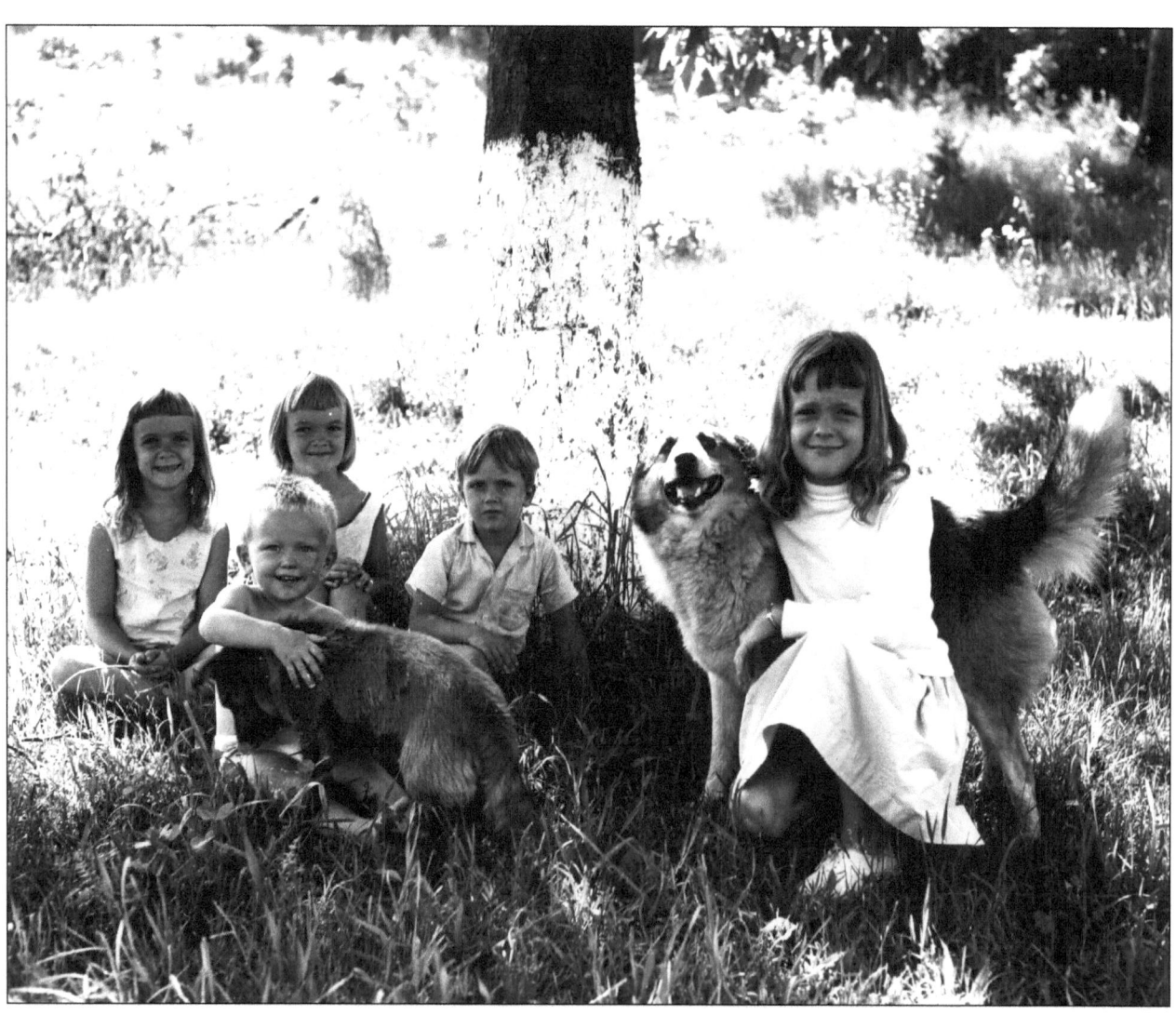

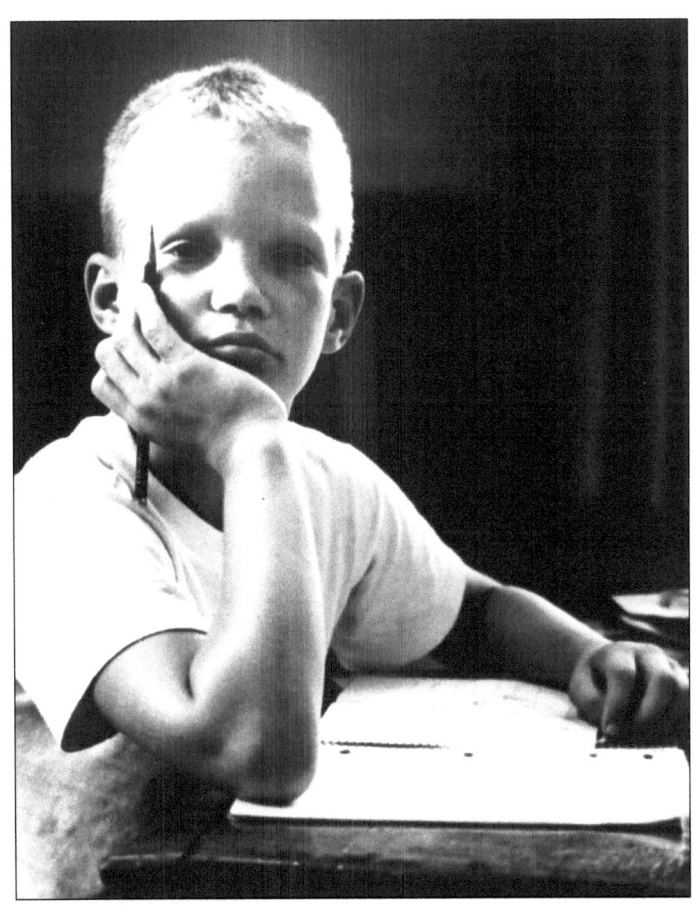

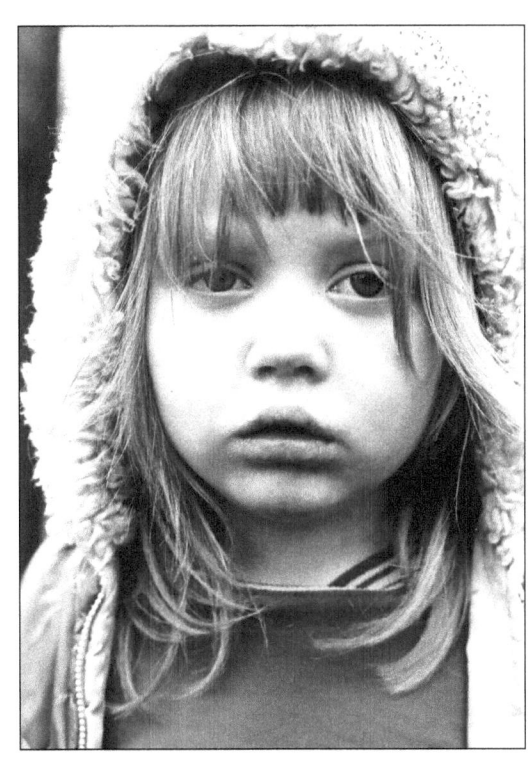

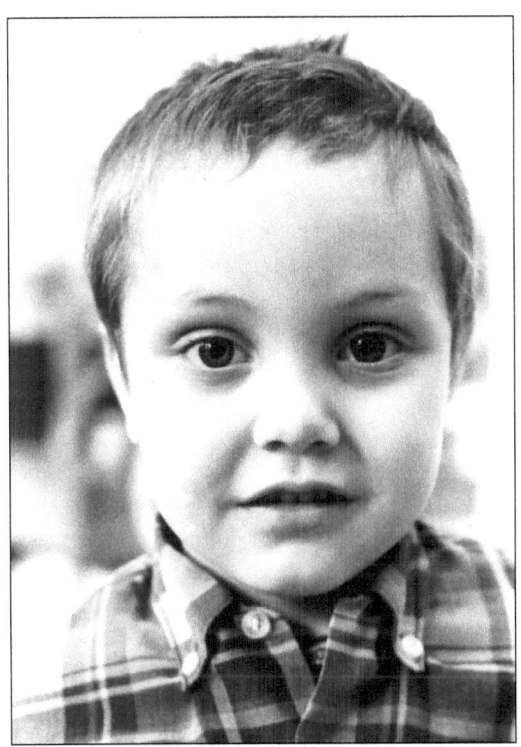

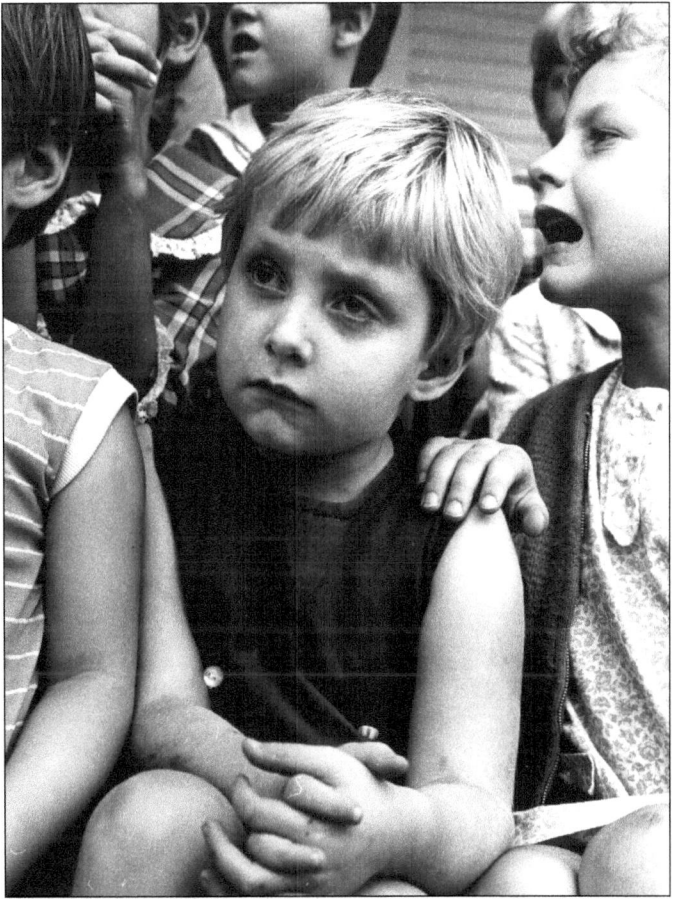

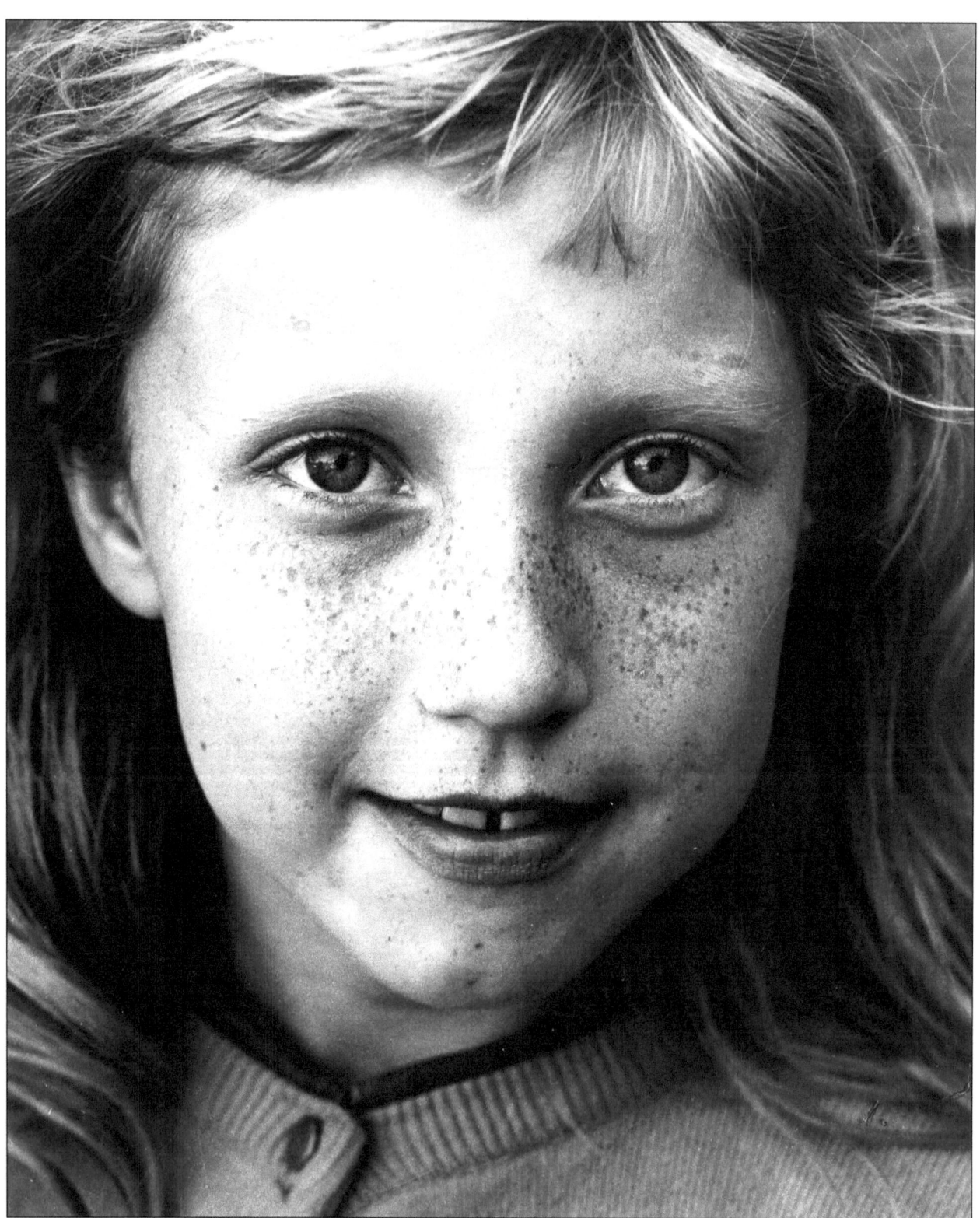

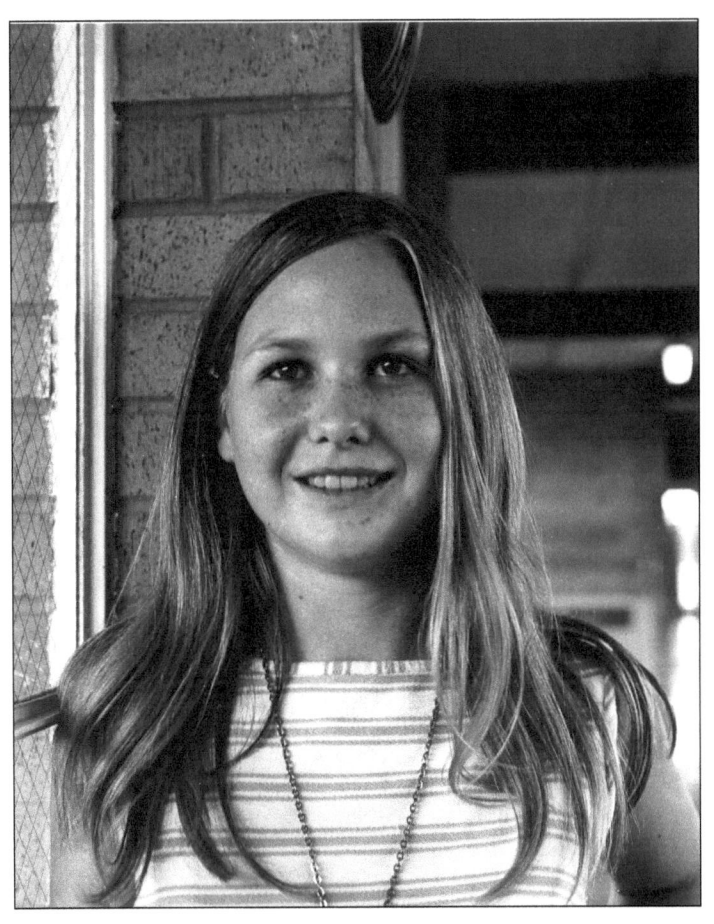

We shall never know all the good that a simple smile can do.
~ **Mother Teresa**

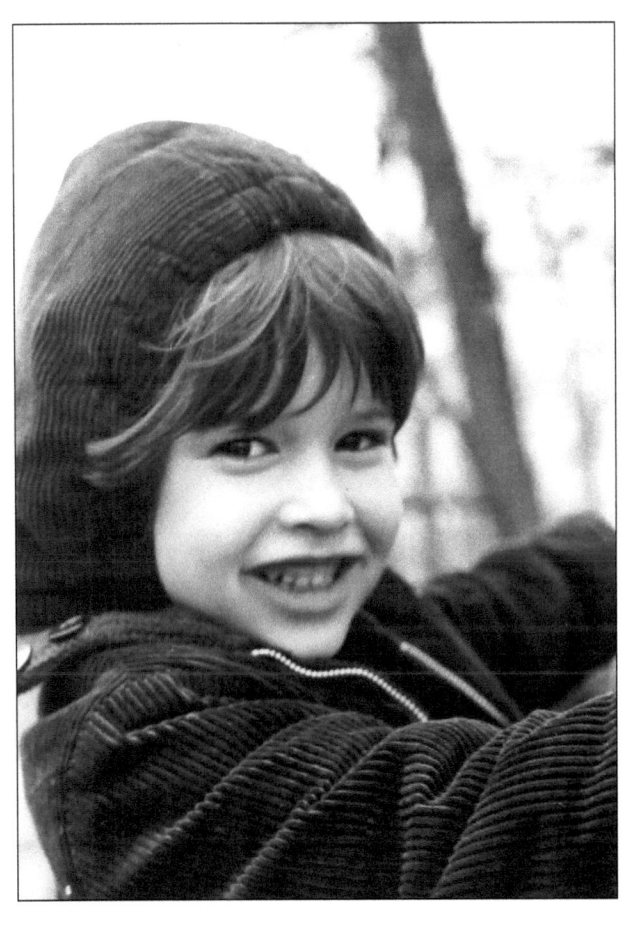

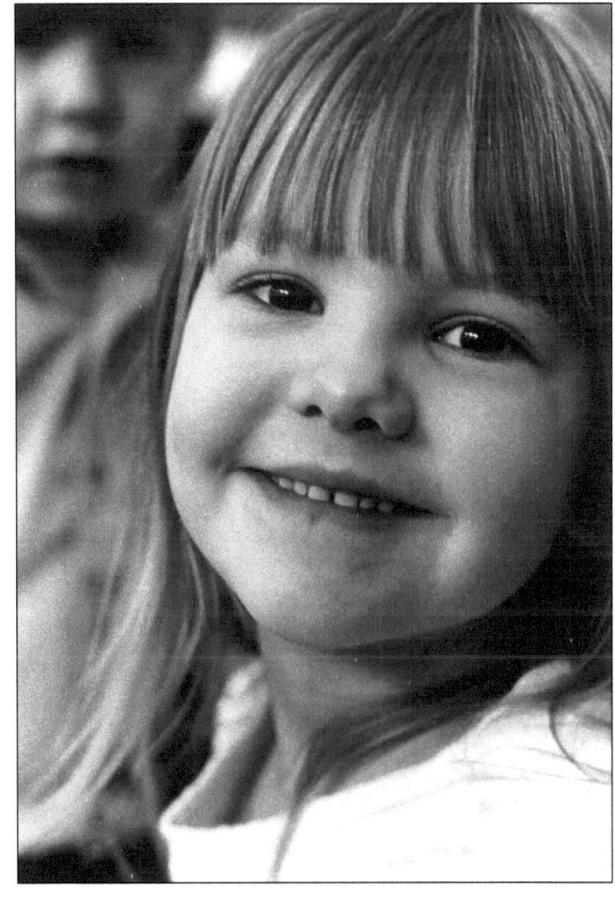

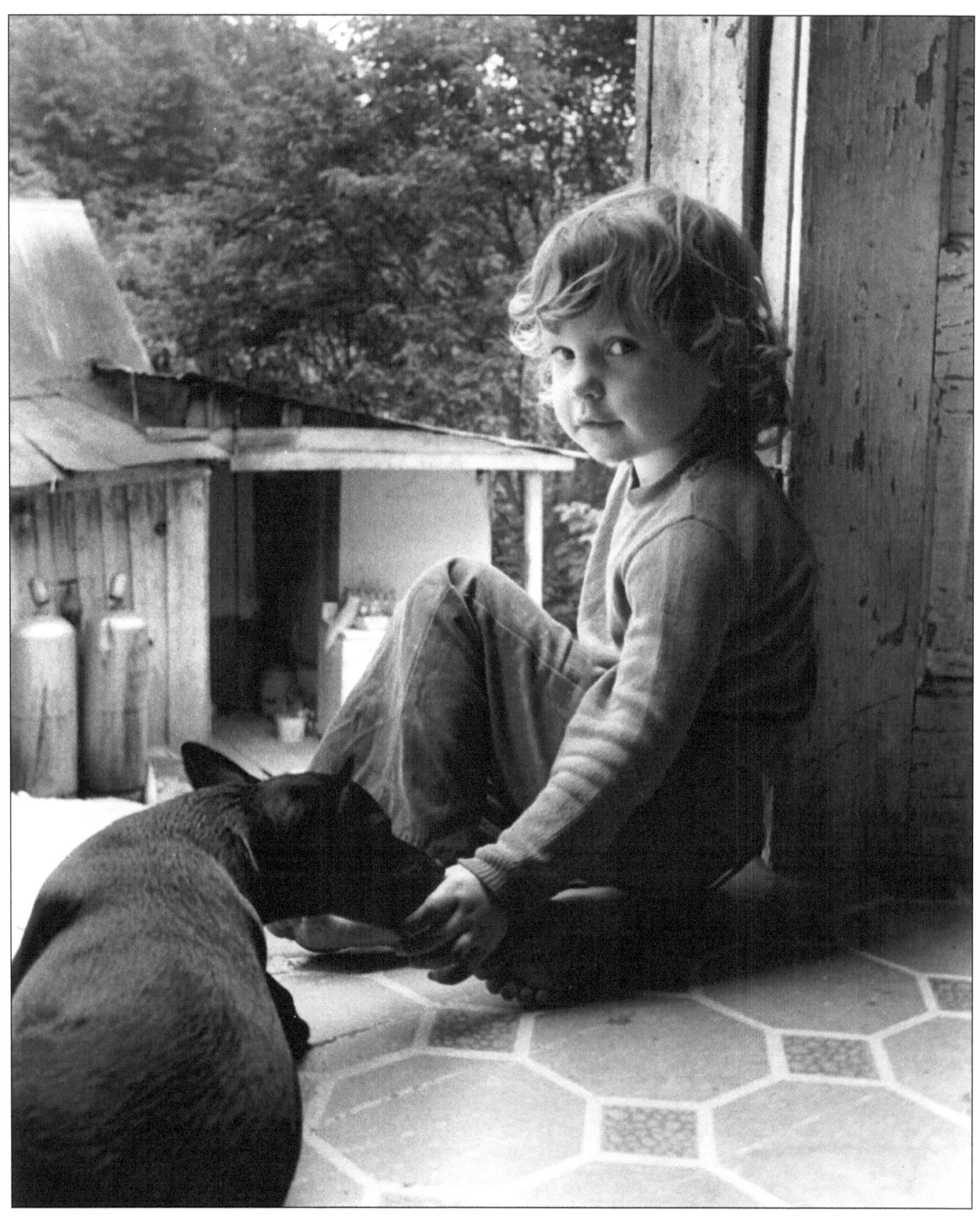

A dog teaches a boy fidelity, perseverance, and to turn around three times before lying down. ~**Robert Benchley**

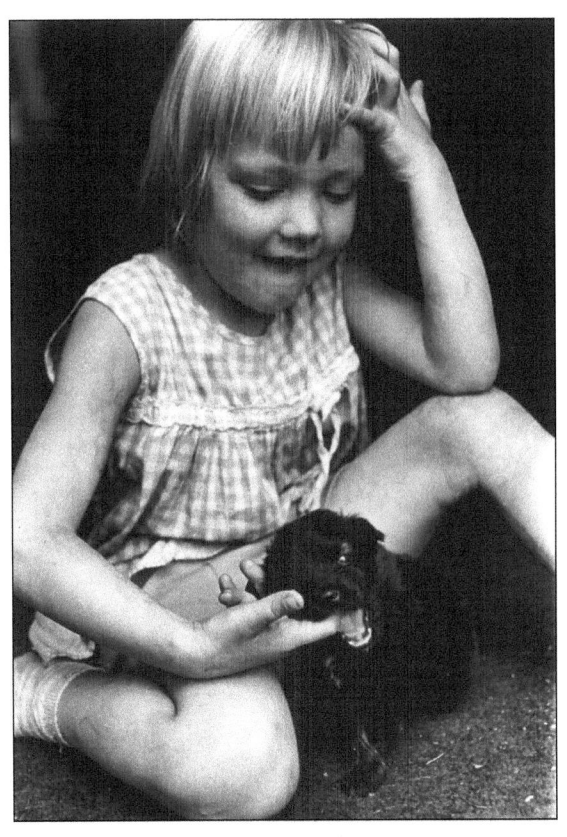
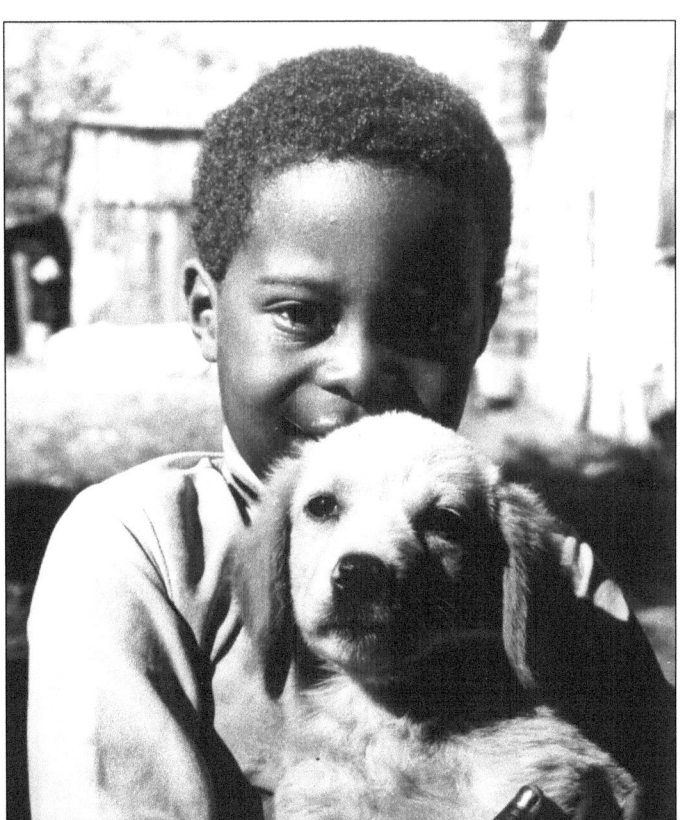

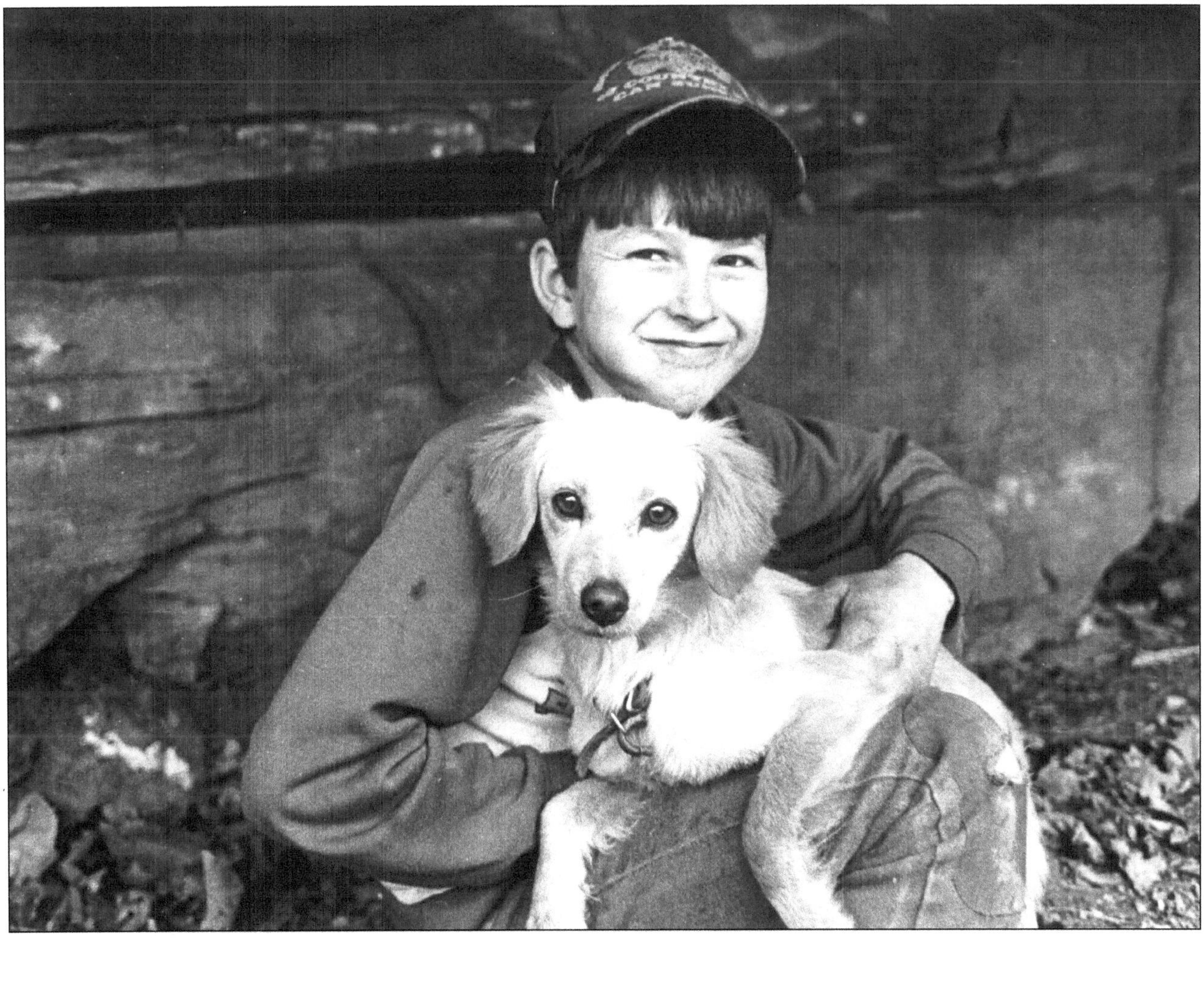

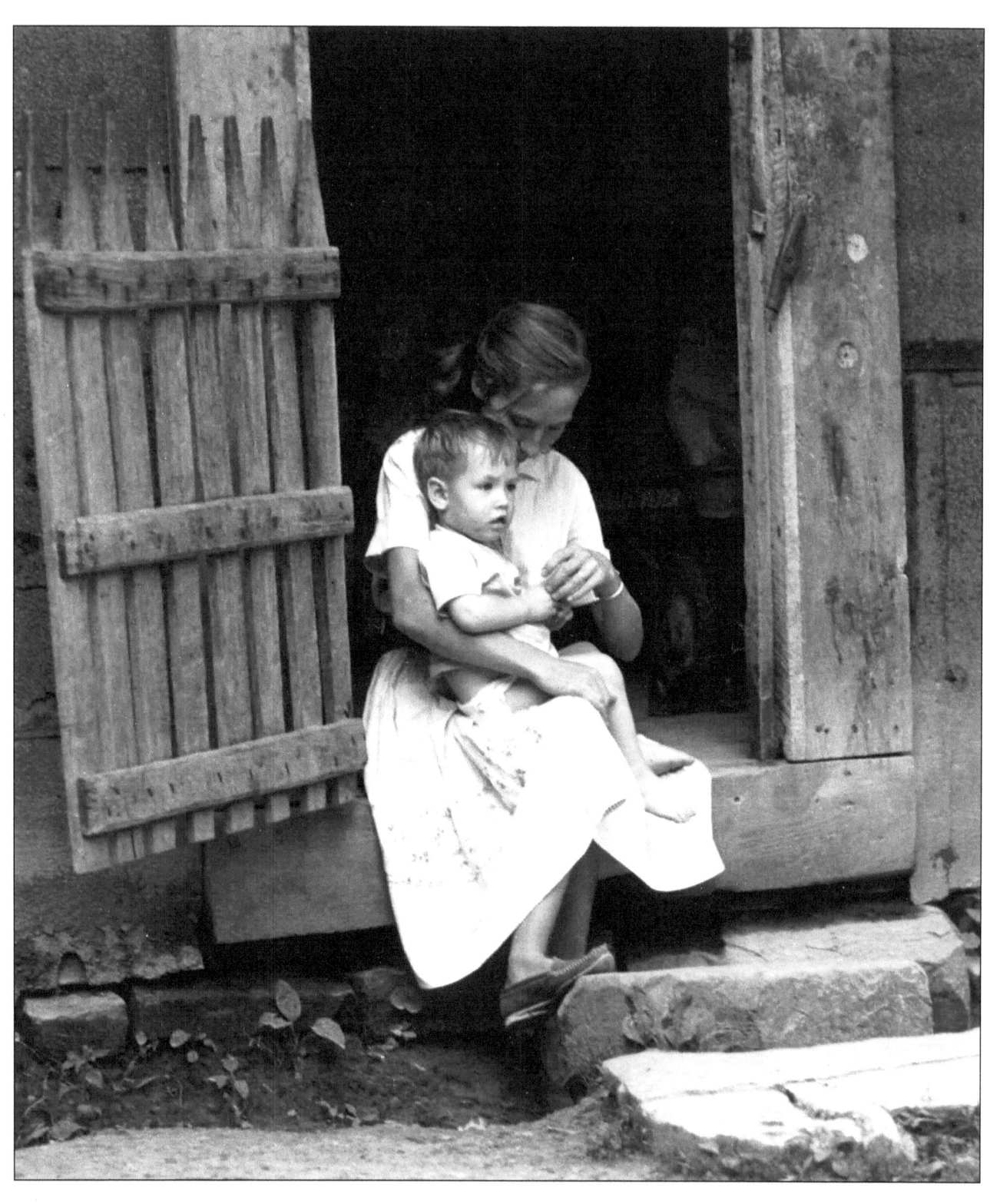

" *The family is one of nature's masterpieces.*
~ **George Santayana** "

He carried his childhood like a hurt warm bird held to his middle-aged breast. ~Herbert Gold

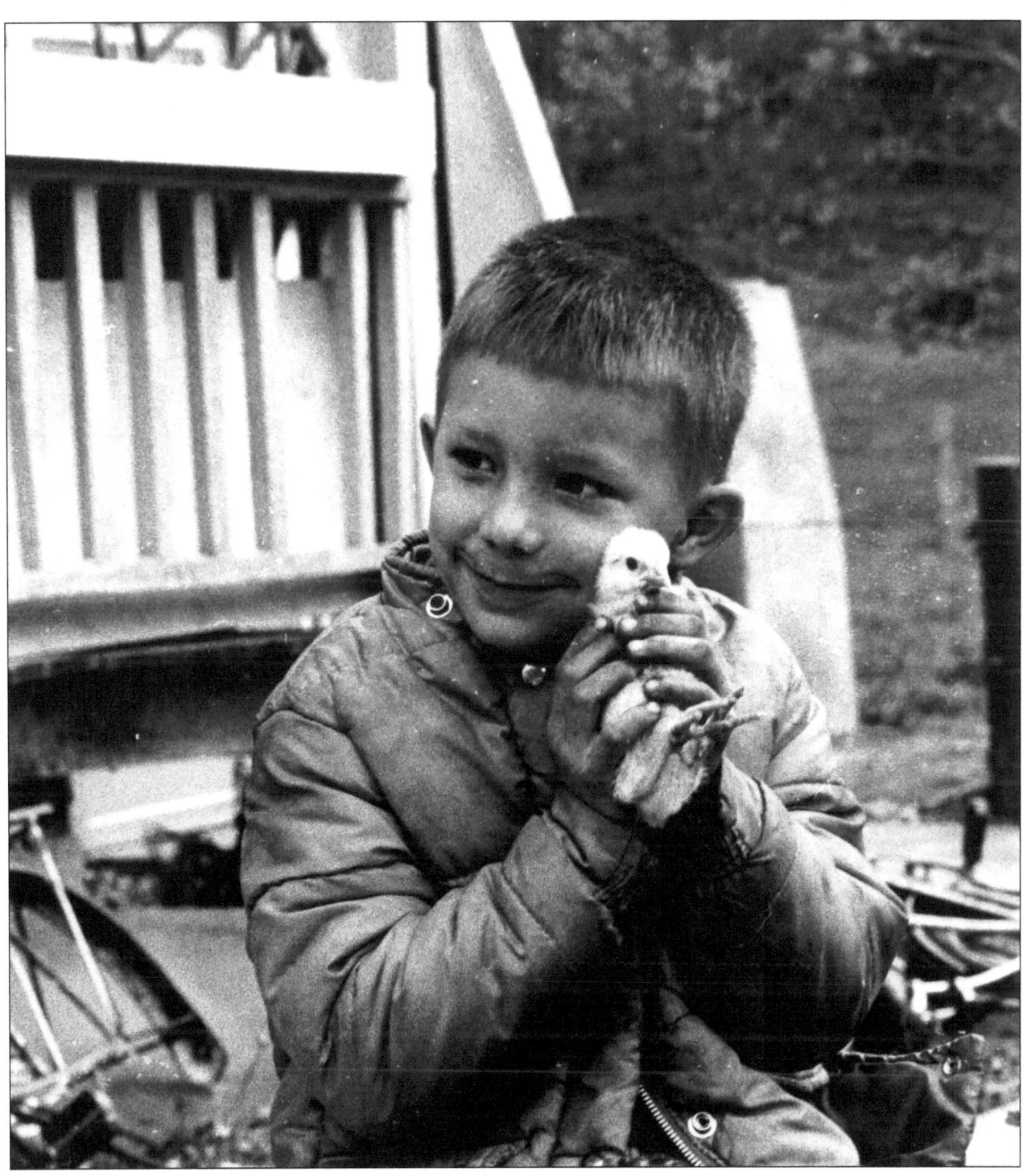

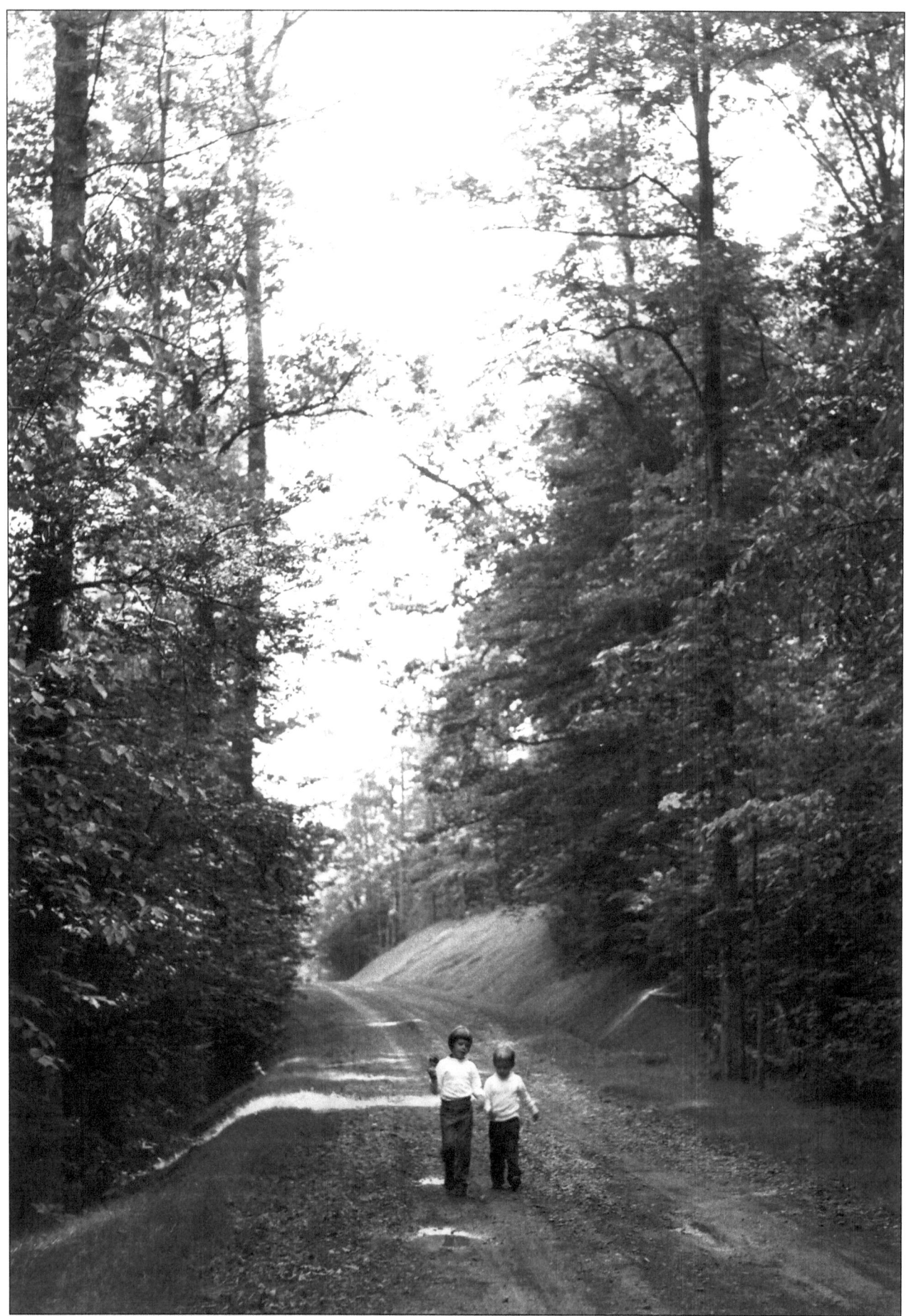

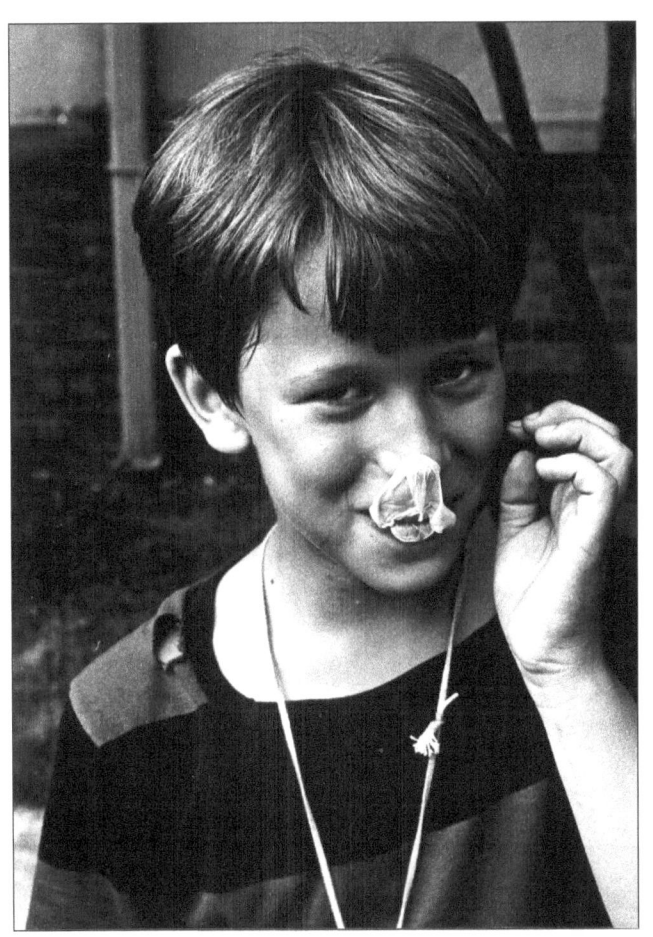

Even when freshly washed and relieved of all obvious confections, children tend to be sticky.

~ Fran Lebowitz

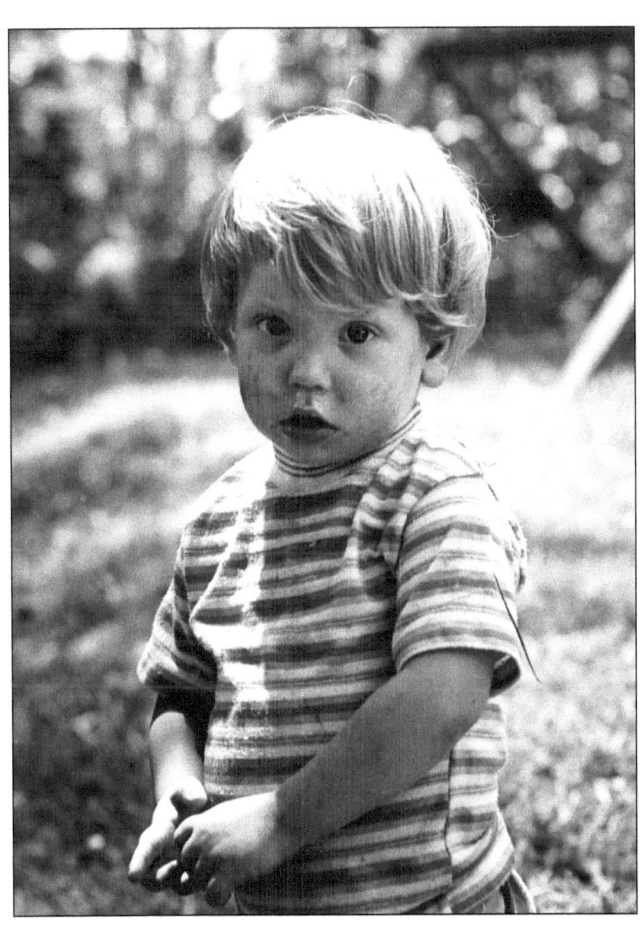

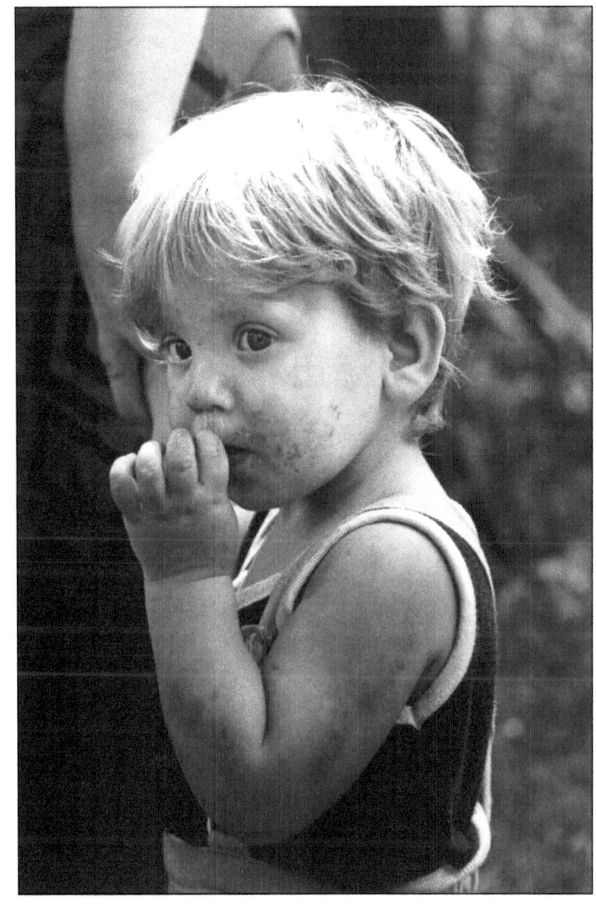

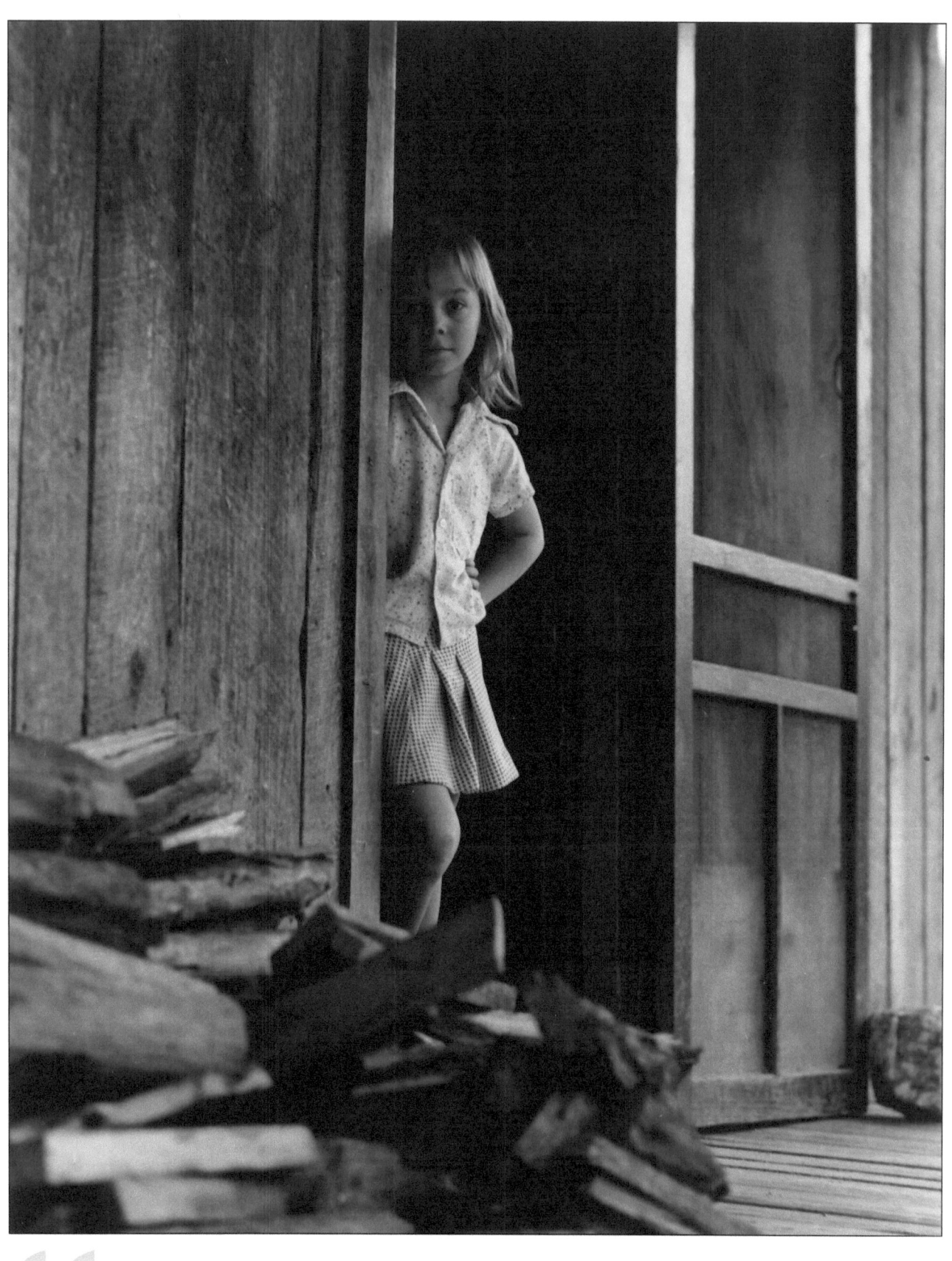

" *There is always one moment in childhood when the door opens and lets the future in.* ~ **Graham Greene** "

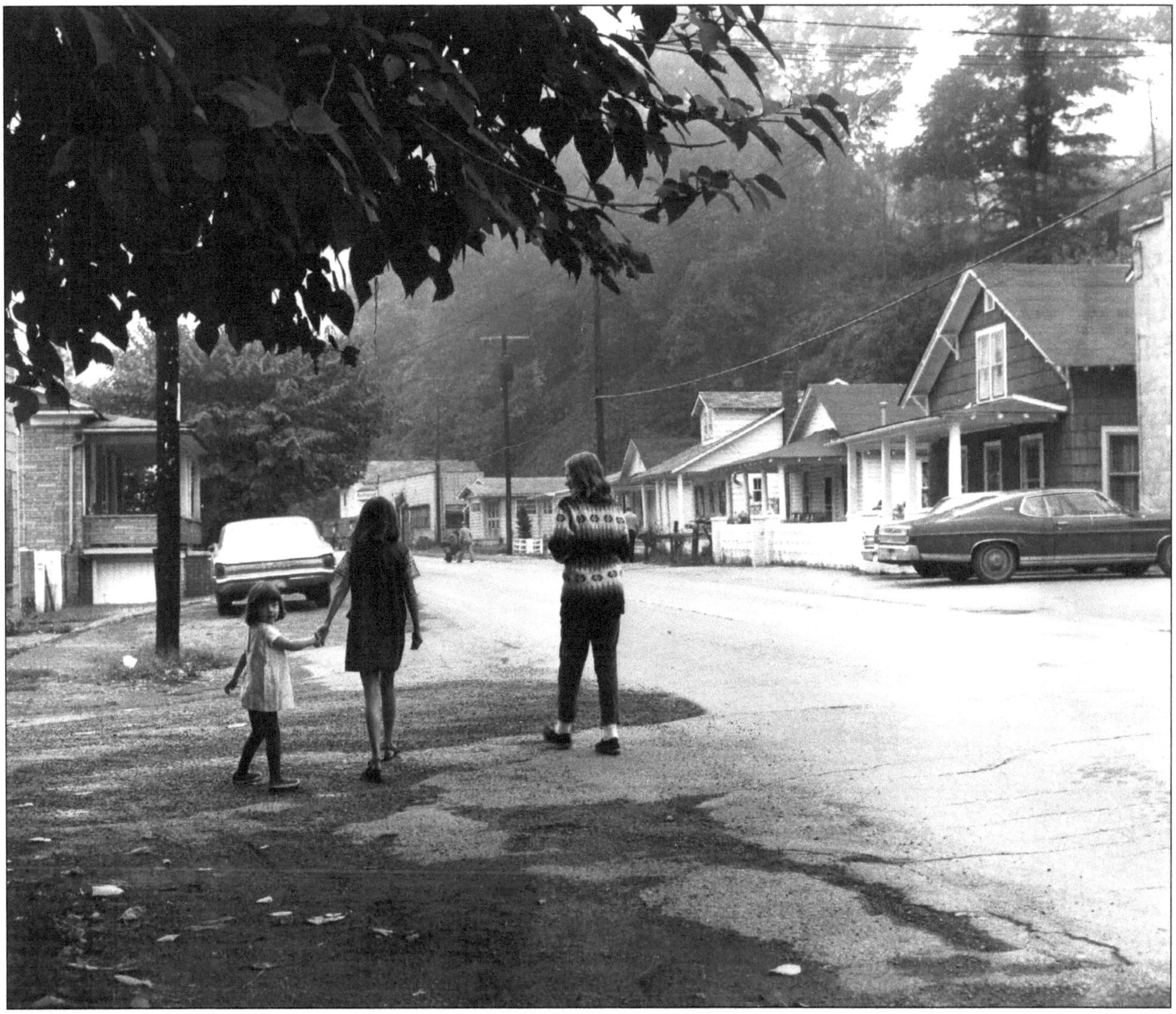

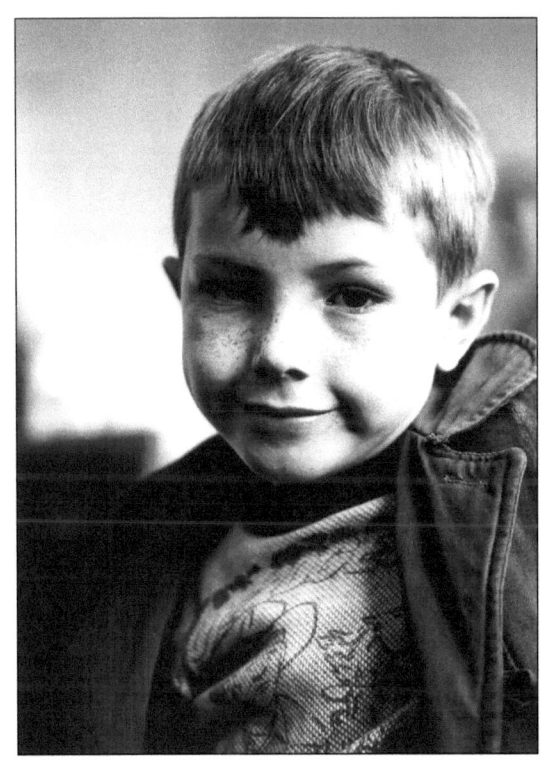

*The nice part about living in
a small town is that when you
don't know what you're doing,
someone else does.*

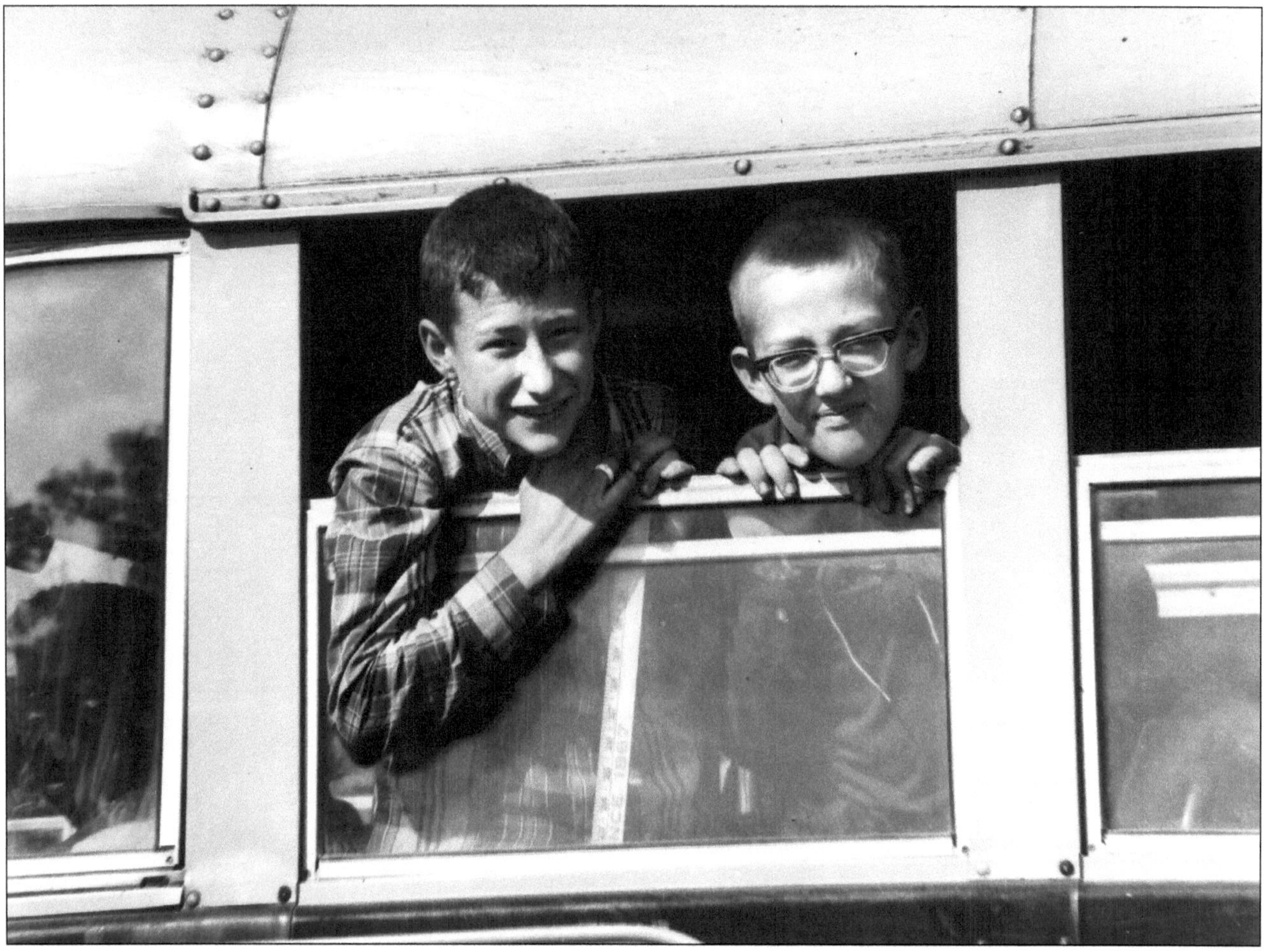

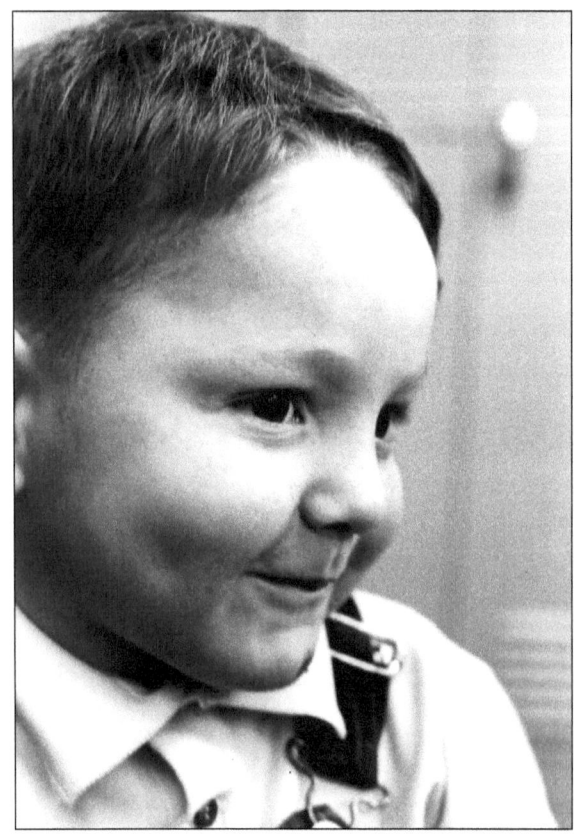
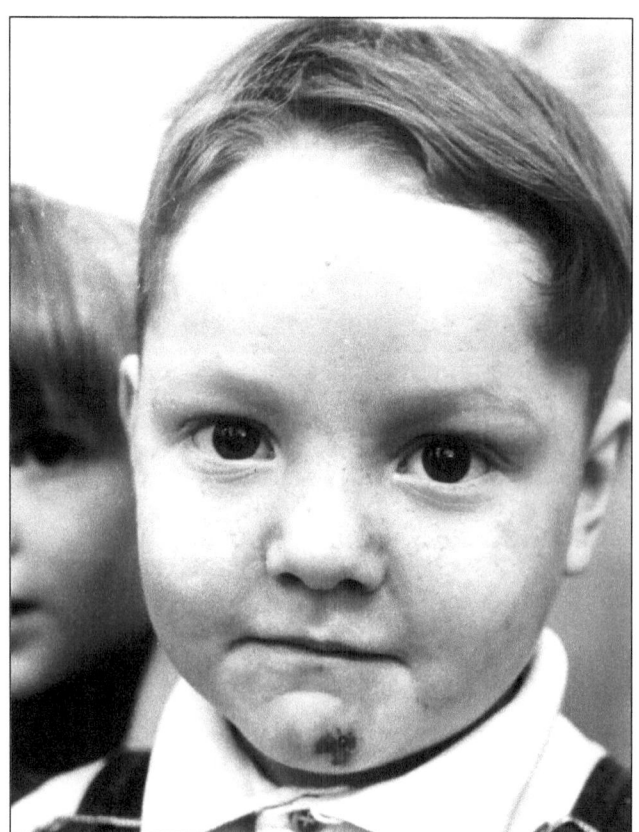

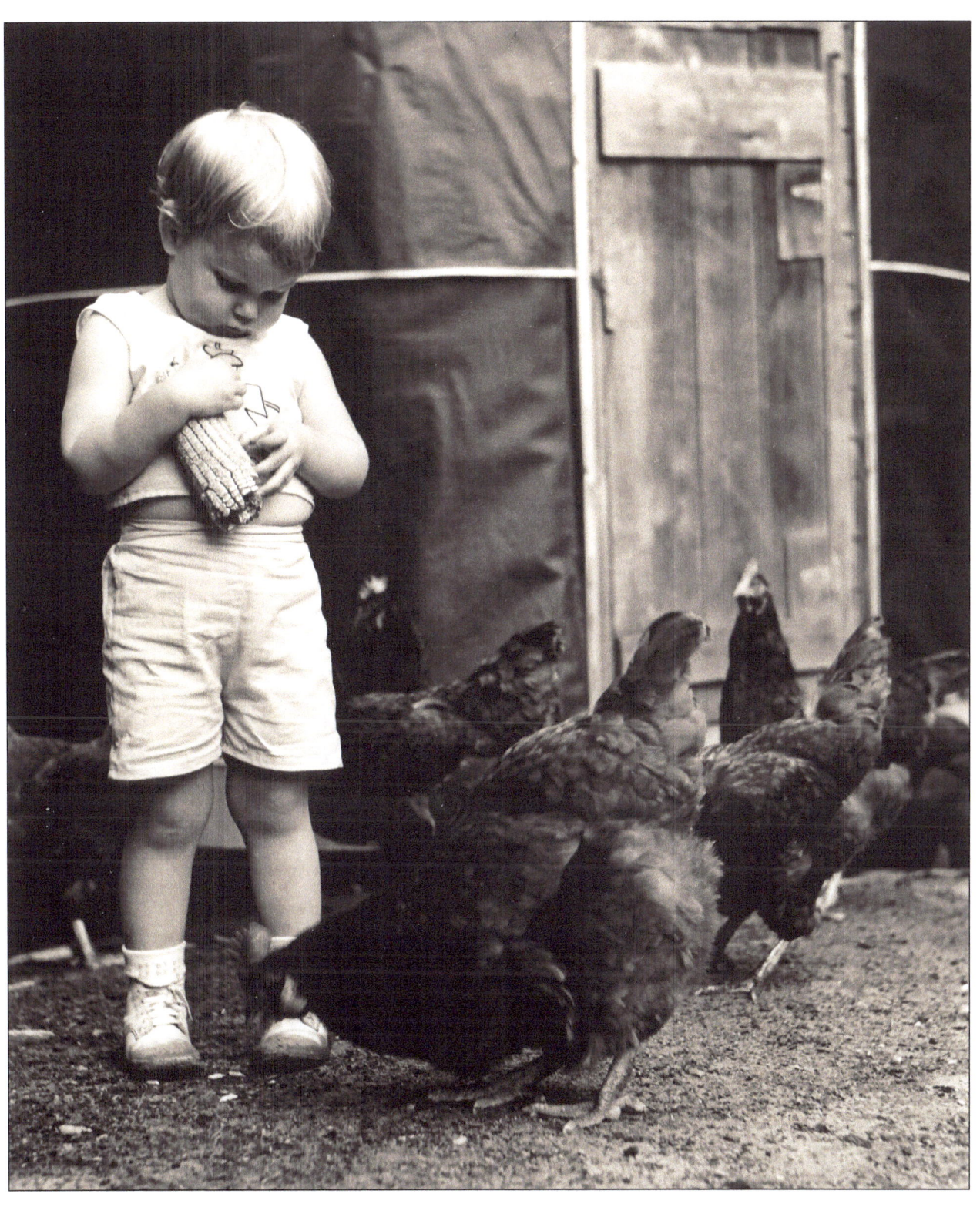

" *I want there to be no peasant in my kingdom so poor that he cannot have a chicken in his pot every Sunday.* ~ **Henry IV** "

I never teach my pupils; I only attempt to provide the conditions in which they can learn.
~ Albert Einstein

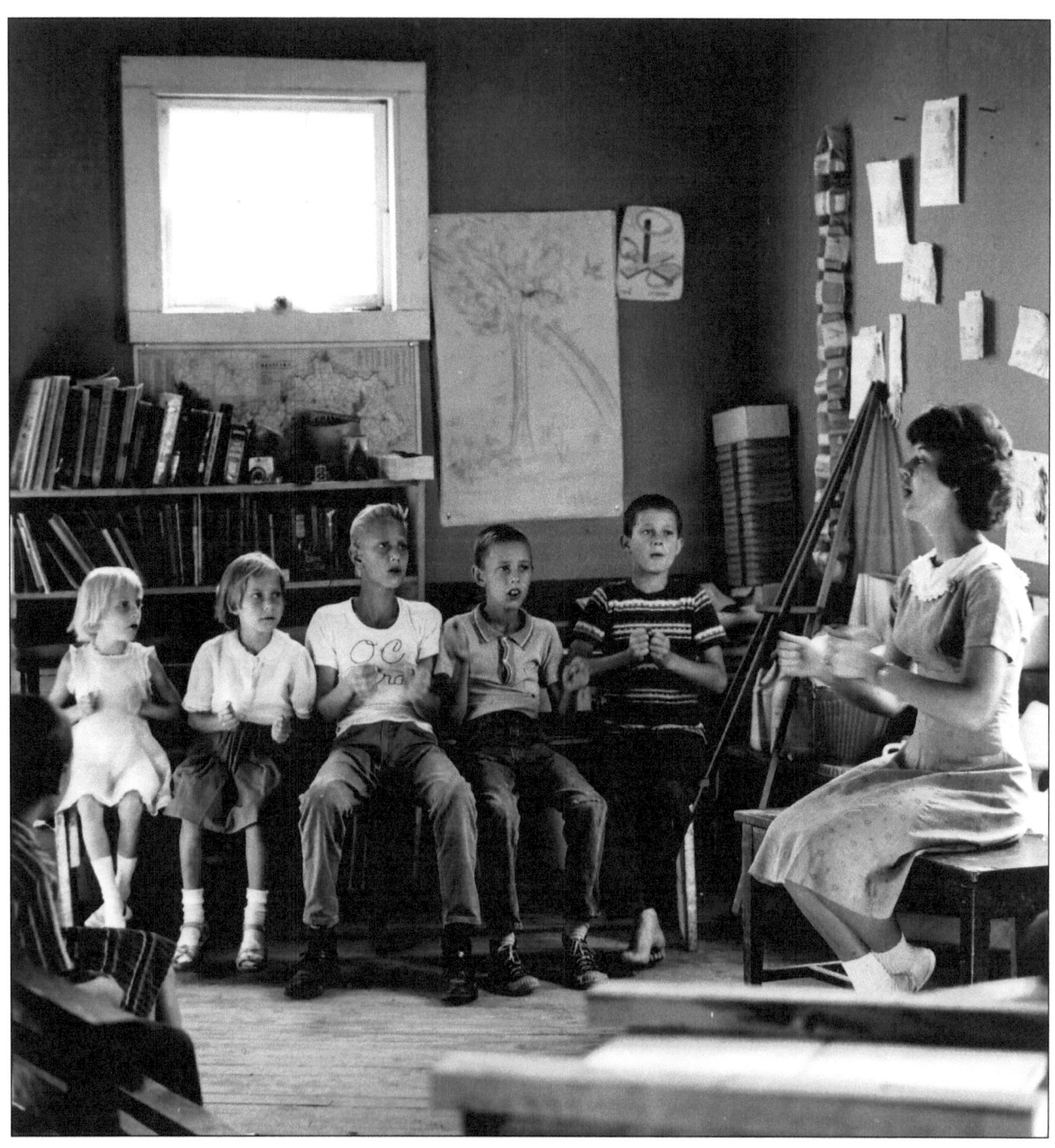

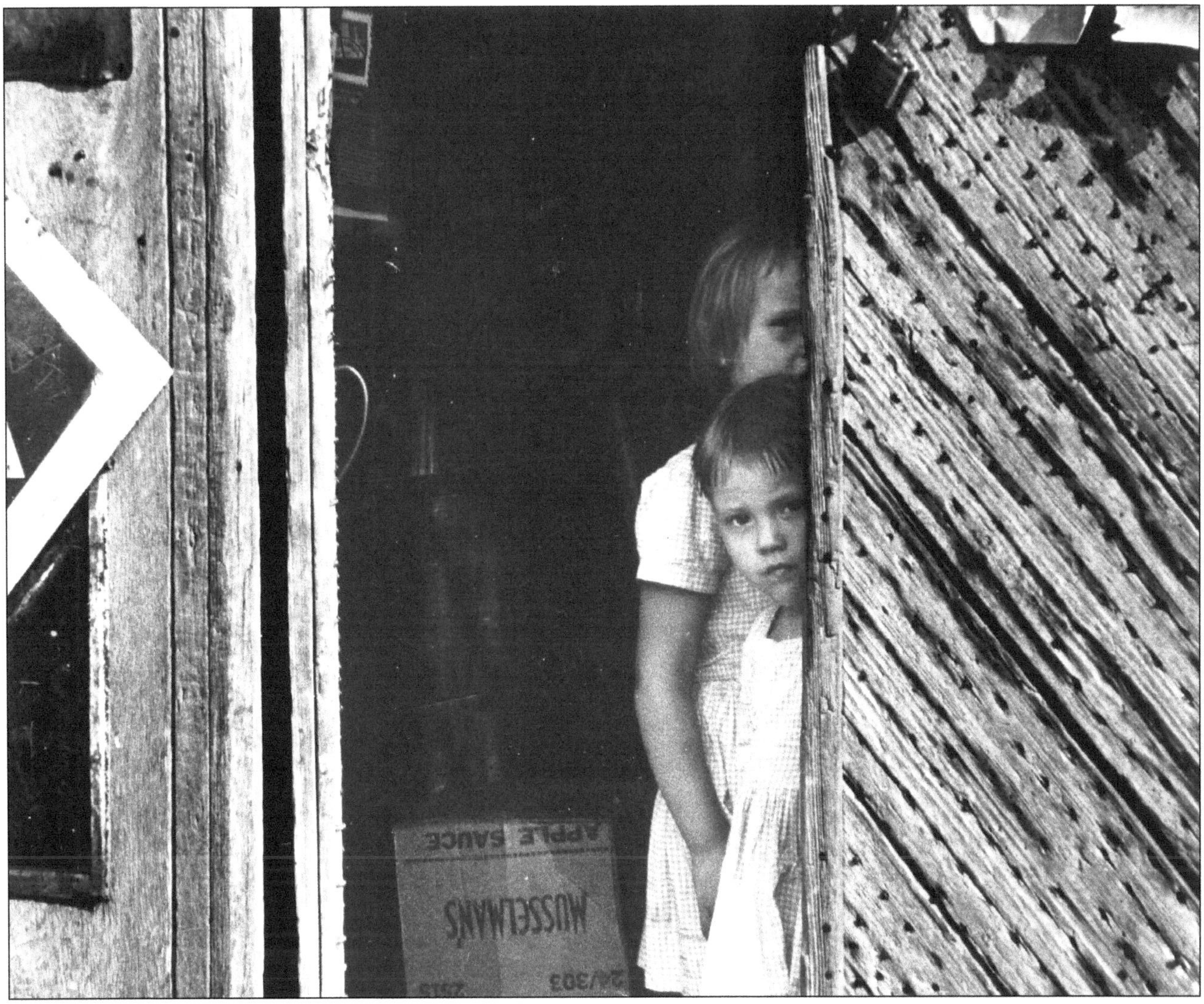

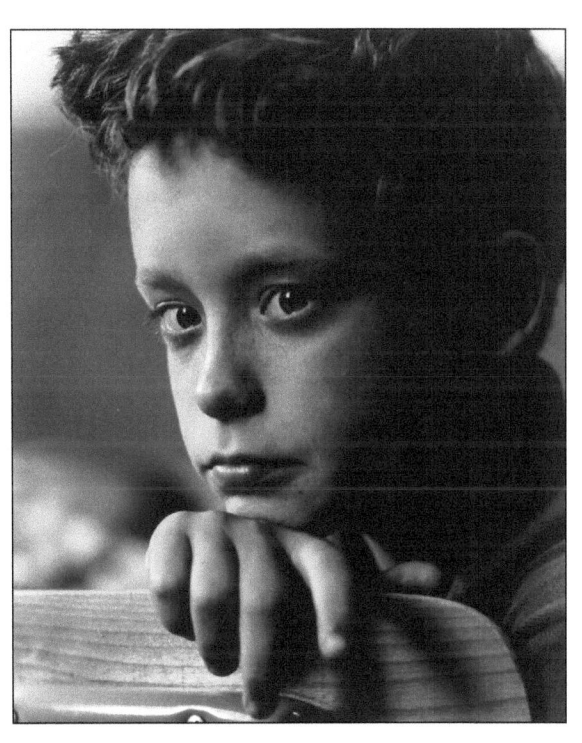

When you follow your bliss... doors will open where you would not have thought there would be doors; and where there wouldn't be a door for anyone else.

~ Joseph Campbell

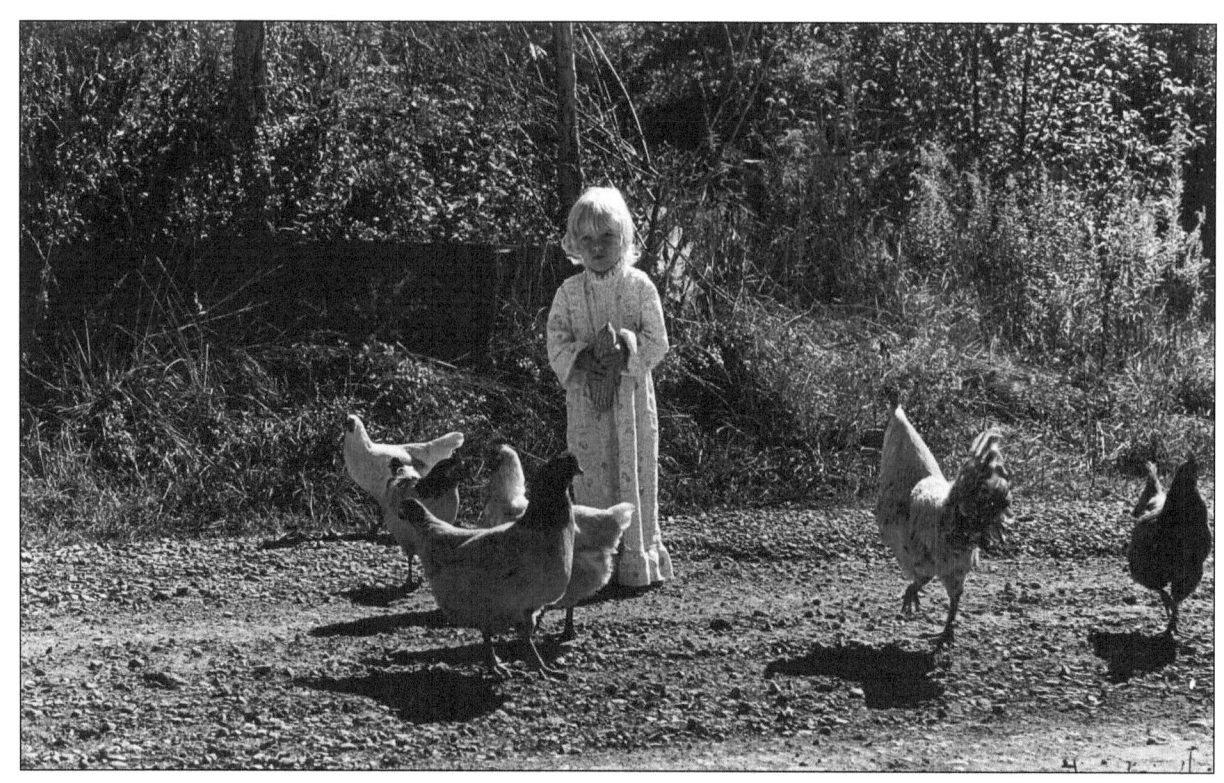

*" The most effective kind of education is that a child should play amongst lovely things. ~ **Plato** "*

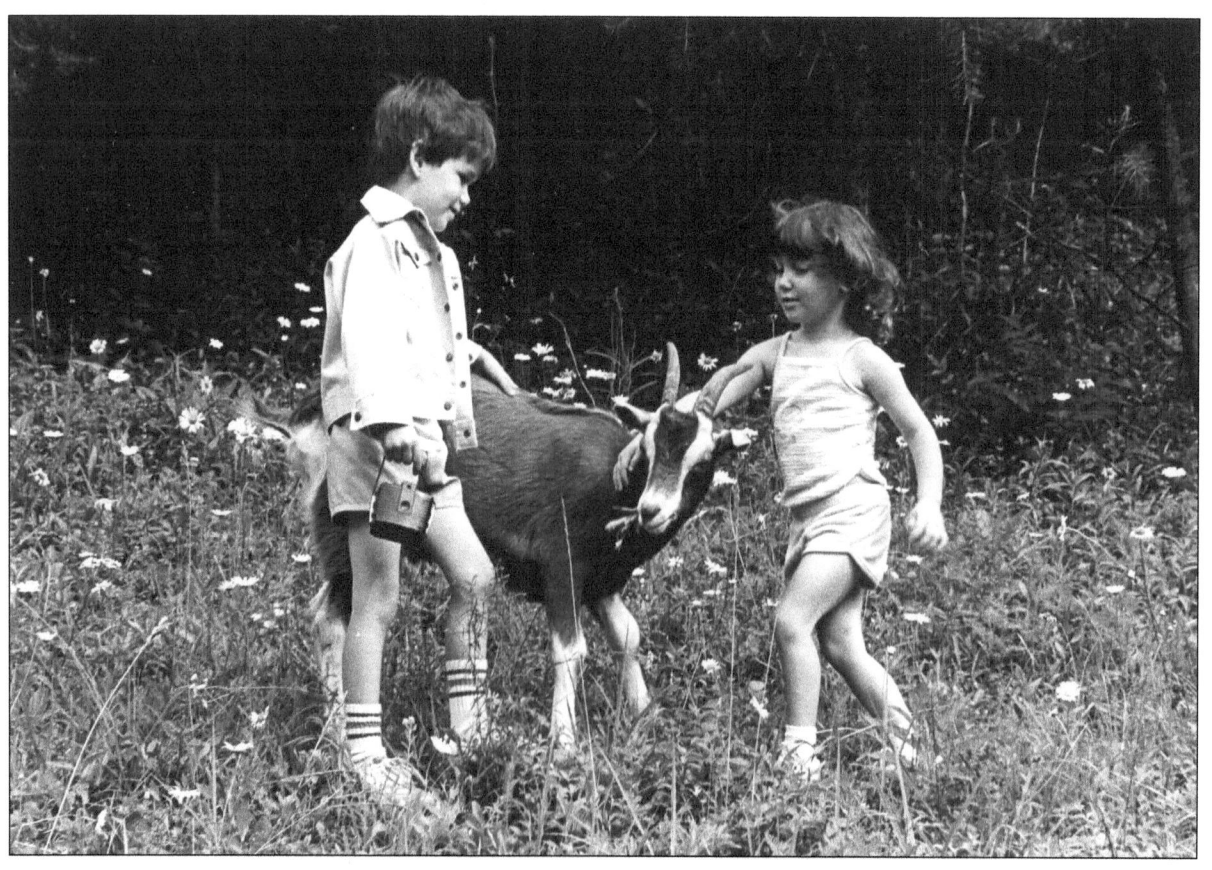

Far and away the best prize that life has to offer is the chance to work hard at work worth doing.
~ **Theodore Roosevelt**

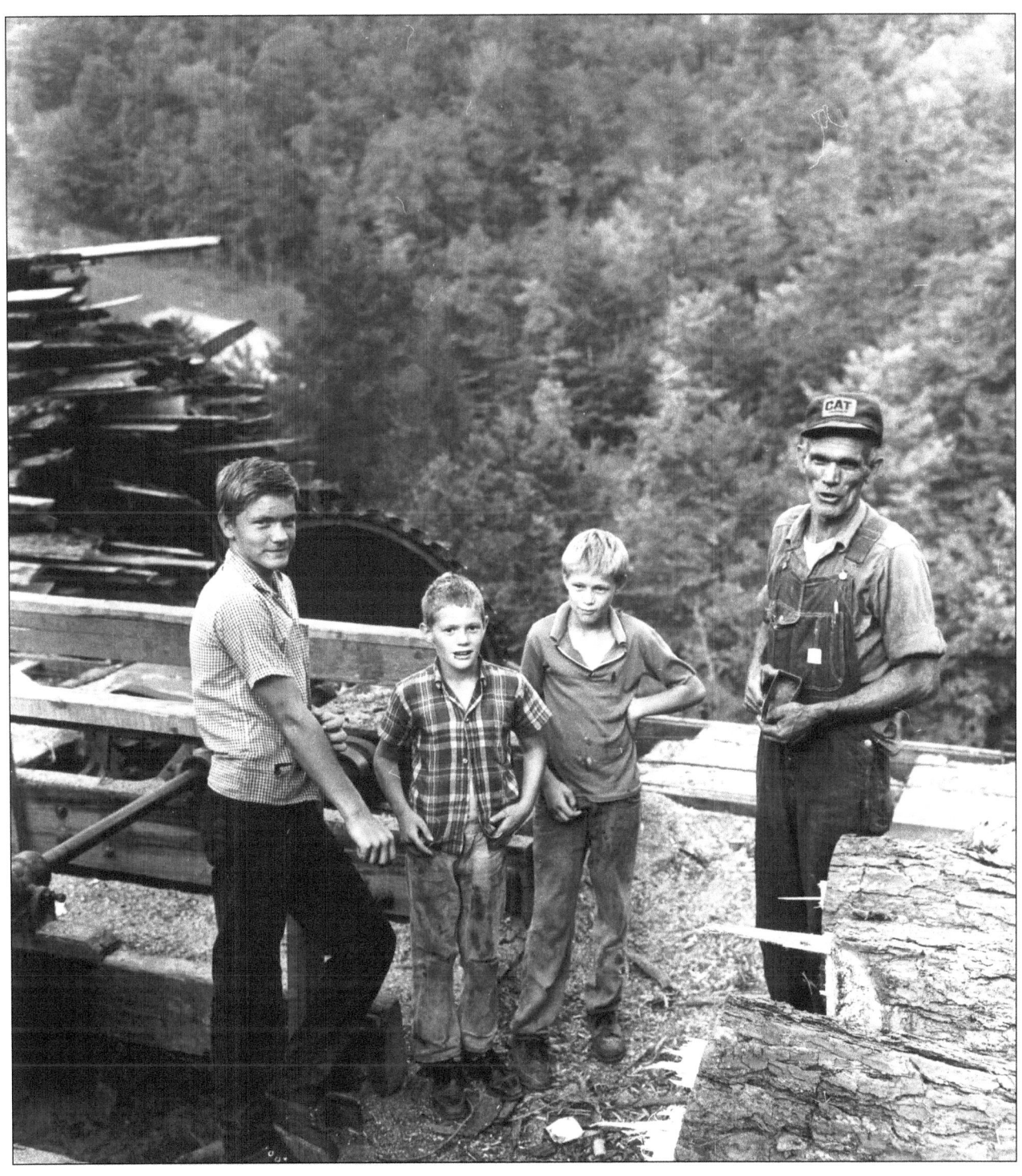

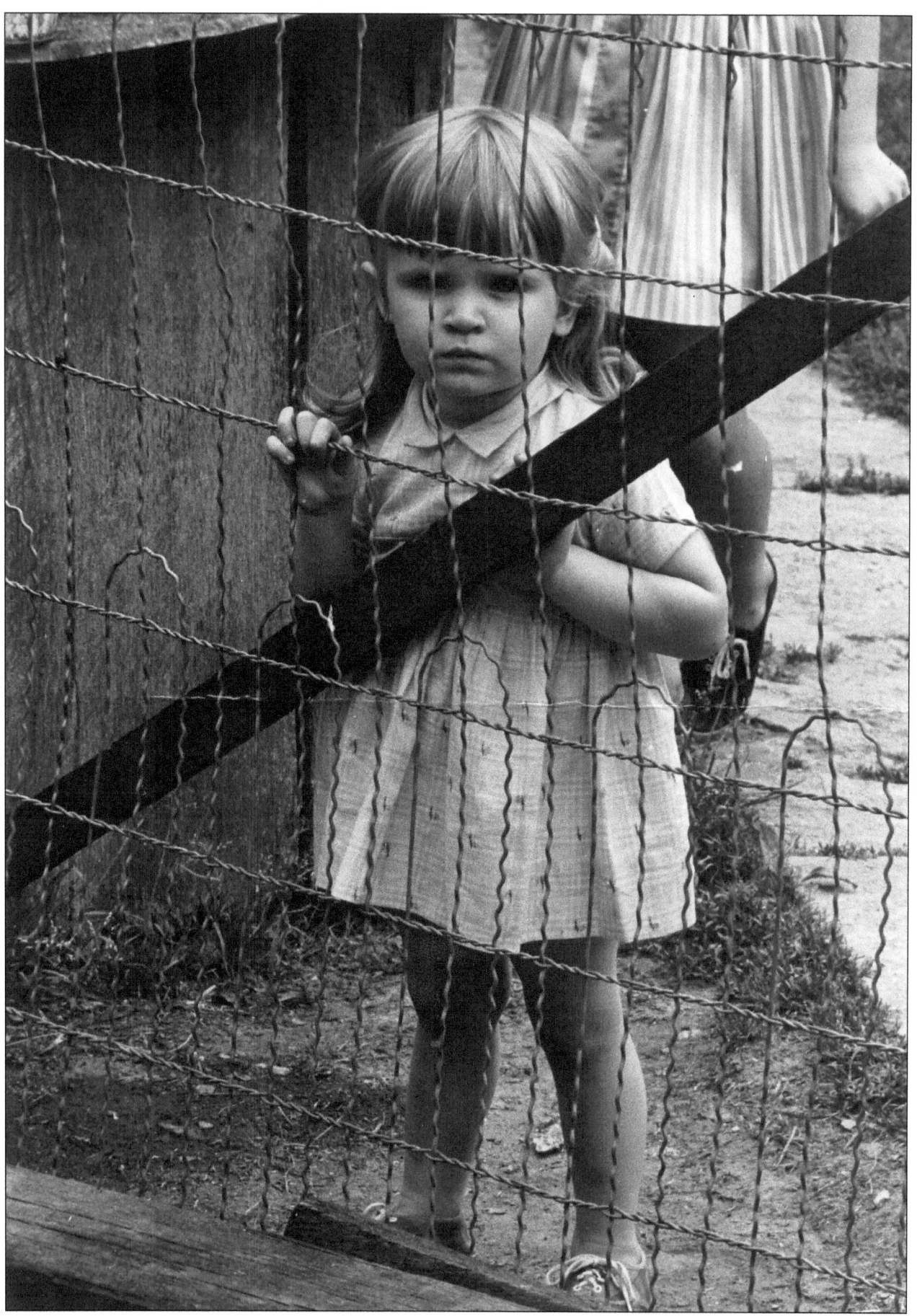

**Brunner Photograph of
Small Appalachian Girl
Inside Tall Wire Fence**

By Grace Freeman

*I am aware night animals
and other dangers
roam your mountains
and the home fence that forms
is meant to keep you safe.
But when the time is right,
will there be a gate?*

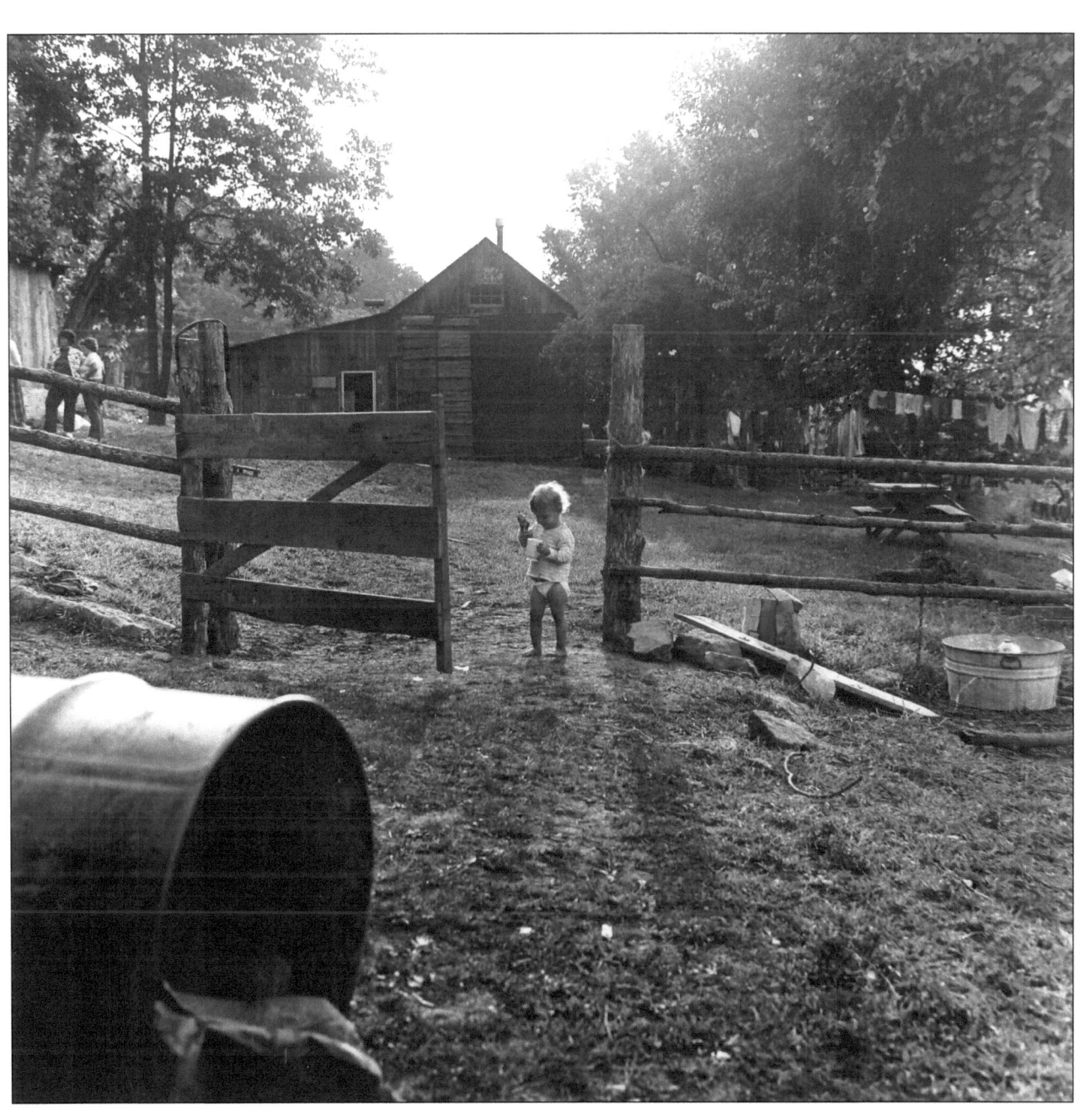